YAS

FRIENDS
OF ACPL

W9-AFQ-516

Methamphetamine

Drugs

Other books in the Compact Research series include:

Drugs

Heroin
Marijuana
Nicotine and Tobacco
Performance Enhancing Drugs

Current Issues

Biomedical Ethics
The Death Penalty
Gun Control
Illegal Immigration
World Energy Crisis

Methamphetamine

by Emma Carlson Berne

Drugs

ReferencePoint
Press™

San Diego, CA

© 2007 ReferencePoint Press, Inc.

For more information, contact
ReferencePoint Press, Inc.
17150 Via del Campo Road, Suite 204
San Diego, CA 92127
www.ReferencePointPress.com

Picture Credits:
Maury Aaseng, 33–35, 47–50, 63, 65
AP/WideWorld Photos, 11, 16
Tamia Dowlatabadi, 32
Mark Sampson, 62, 64, 79–81

Series design:
 Tamia Dowlatabadi

LIBRARY OF CONGRESS CATALOGING-IN-PUBLICATION DATA

Berne, Emma Carlson.
 Methamphetamine / Emma Carlson Berne.
   p. cm. — (Compact research series)
 Includes bibliographical references and index.
 ISBN-13: 978-1-60152-004-3 (alk. paper)
 ISBN-10: 1-60152-004-2 (alk. paper)
 1. Methamphetamine abuse—Juvenile literature. I. Title.
RC568.A45B47 2006
362.29'9—dc22

2006032206

Contents

Foreword

❝Where is the knowledge we have lost in information?❞

—"The Rock," T.S. Eliot

A s modern civilization continues to evolve, its ability to create, store, distribute, and access information expands exponentially. The explosion of information from all media continues to increase at a phenomenal rate. By 2020, some experts predict the worldwide information base will double every seventy-three days. While access to diverse sources of information and perspectives is paramount to any democratic society, information alone cannot help people gain knowledge and understanding. Information must be organized and presented clearly and succinctly in order to be understood. The challenge in the digital age becomes not the creation of information, but how best to sort, organize, enhance, and present information.

ReferencePoint Press developed the Compact Research series with this challenge of the information age in mind. More than any other subject area today, researching current events can yield vast, diverse, and unqualified information that can be intimidating and overwhelming for even the most advanced and motivated researcher. The Compact Research series offers a compact, relevant, intelligent, and conveniently organized collection of information covering a variety of current and controversial topics ranging from illegal immigration to marijuana.

The series focuses on three types of information: objective single-author narratives, opinion-based primary source quotations, and facts and statistics. The clearly written objective narratives provide context and reliable background information. Primary source quotes are carefully selected and cited, exposing the reader to differing points of view. And facts and statistics sections aid the reader in evaluating perspectives. Presenting these key types of information creates a richer, more balanced learning experience.

For better understanding and convenience, the series enhances information by organizing it into narrower topics and adding design features that make it easy for a reader to identify desired content. For example, in *Compact Research: Illegal Immigration*, a chapter covering the economic impact of illegal immigration has an objective narrative explaining the various ways the economy is impacted, a balanced section of fifteen primary source quotes on the topic, followed by facts and full-color illustrations to encourage evaluation of contrasting perspectives.

The ancient Roman philosopher Lucius Annaeus Seneca wrote, "It is quality rather than quantity that matters." More than just a collection of content, the Compact Research series is simply committed to creating, finding, organizing, and presenting the most relevant and appropriate amount of information on a current topic in a user-friendly style that invites, intrigues, and fosters understanding.

Methamphetamine at a Glance

Prevalence

Methamphetamine is the most widely used synthetic drug in America. According to the U.S. Department of Health and Human Services, 1.5 million Americans are regular meth users.

Addiction

The key ingredients in methamphetamine, ephedrine and pseudo-ephedrine, combine with other ingredients to form a highly addictive stimulant.

Difficulty of Addiction Prevention

Meth addiction is particularly hard to prevent because of the intensely pleasurable high the drug initially creates. Users quickly become both physically and psychologically addicted.

Health Dangers

Meth permanently damages blood vessels, leading to strokes and heart attacks. Long-term meth use also destroys cells in the pleasure center of the brain and creates a motor disorder similar to Parkinson's disease.

Manufacture

Control of meth-making labs is difficult because the drug can be made in small home setups using ordinary household equipment.

Hazards of Meth Making

Meth labs are dangerous to those cooking the drug and those living near the lab. The toxic chemicals and high temperatures needed to manufacture the drug frequently result in noxious fumes, explosions, and fires.

Laws

States are trying to control meth abuse by restricting its ingredients. As of 2006, thirty-five states have passed legislation controlling pseudoephedrine and ephedrine.

Overview

Methamphetamine is a highly addictive stimulant drug that is chemically manufactured from a variety of common household ingredients. It affects the brain and central nervous system, creating a euphoric high. Methamphetamine is related to amphetamine, which is a stimulant drug created by the pharmaceutical industry to treat obesity and increase wakefulness. Slang names for methamphetamine include meth, speed, tina, chalk, glass, ice, crank, crissy, and crystal.

Meth is the fastest-growing illegal drug in the United States. As of 2005, over 12 million Americans had used methamphetamine at least once and 1.5 million were considered addicts. By comparison, only 7.8 million had tried crack cocaine at least once, and only 3.1 million had tried heroin. The number of methamphetamine addicts who entered drug rehabilitation clinics in 2002 was up 119 percent from 1995.

Help with Staying Alert

Methamphetamine is a synthetic drug; its ingredients are entirely man-made, as opposed to plant-based drugs such as cocaine or heroin, which are made from coca and poppies, respectively. The drug was first synthesized by Japanese chemists in 1919 and was given to pilots in World War II to help them stay awake during long missions. It was considered quite safe. Methamphetamine's predecessor, the less potent amphetamine,

One hit of methamphetamine can get a user high for days. This bag contains one ounce of crystal methamphetamine.

was frequently prescribed under the brand name Benzedrine during the 1940s and 1950s for depression, alertness, and weight loss. Not realizing the high potential for harmful abuse, doctors frequently overprescribed the drug. President John F. Kennedy frequently took amphetamines during his presidency to help him with alertness and back pain.

Congress made both amphetamine and methamphetamine illegal without a prescription in 1970. At that time illicit use of the drug was centered almost entirely on the West Coast. California motorcycle gangs had begun distributing the drug, transporting it in their crankcases—leading to the popular nickname "crank." Abuse of the drug spread quickly through California, to Oregon and Washington, and to Hawaii. During the 1970s and 1980s, public attention was focused on cocaine and crack cocaine, and penalties for use of those drugs were stiff. Dealers needed another drug to satisfy their customers, and meth, distributed through the well-established cocaine system, seemed to fit the bill nicely: It was cheap, easy to manufacture, relatively unknown to authorities, and best of all, highly addictive. By the mid-1990s, illicit methamphetamine use had started to move eastward from the West Coast to the western and midwestern states. It quickly became popular among blue-collar workers living in isolated rural communities as a way to stay awake for long shifts and even longer commutes across the vast spaces of the plains states.

Key Ingredients

Today, the Drug Enforcement Administration classifies methamphetamine as a Schedule II drug, the second most severe rating under the federal Controlled Substances Act. The most severe is Schedule I, those drugs which have no accepted medical use in the United States, such as heroin and LSD. Schedule II drugs are those that have a high potential for abuse but are still medically legal with severe restrictions. Morphine, PCP, methadone, and cocaine are other Schedule II drugs. Methamphetamine is occasionally prescribed in small, carefully monitored doses to treat obesity, attention deficit disoder, and narcolepsy, a condition characterised by excessive sleepiness. The legal form of the drug is far less potent than the illegal form.

> **Today, the Drug Enforcement Administration classifies methamphetamine as a Schedule II drug, the second most severe rating under the federal Controlled Substances Act.**

The key ingredient in methamphetamine is the chemical pseudoephedrine or its cousin, ephedrine. Pseudoephedrine in particular is found in common cold and allergy medicines such as Sudafed, Claritin, or Benadryl, where it acts as a decongestant by shrinking the blood vessels in the nose and sinuses. When used in methamphetamine, pseudoephedrine and ephedrine are called "precursor chemicals." Meth "cooks" process the ephedrine or pseudoephedrine by combining it with other easily available ingredients over high temperatures to distill the chemicals into a potent form.

Powder and Rock

Methamphetamine generally comes in two forms: powder and rock. Depending on the ingredients used, it can be yellow, brown, gray, orange, pink, or white. "Street meth" is an odorless, bitter-tasting powder that can be snorted, eaten, dissolved in a liquid and drunk, or melted and injected. "Crystal meth" is the purer rock form, usually smoked in a pipe similar to that used for crack cocaine or heated to a liquid and injected. Meth can also be taken in a suppository form, called a "booty bump," or by inhaling the vapors of the powder heated in a bowl—a "hot rail." The hot rail is a very potent method since the chemical goes straight to the lungs. Most users start out snorting or eating meth powder and progress gradually to injecting, which gives the most powerful high.

Methamphetamine use releases high levels of the chemical dopamine in the brain, causing a high. Dopamine is a neurotransmitter which, when released in large amounts, stimulates the brain's pleasure and reward centers and floods the user with feelings of ecstasy and euphoria. Normally, dopamine is released when a person has an ordinary pleasurable experience, such as eating or having sex. A hit of methamphetamine releases up to 12 times as much dopamine as a person would get naturally. Sex, for instance, releases about 150 units of dopamine. Cocaine releases about 350. Meth, on the other hand, creates a veritable dopamine geyser. It releases 1,200 dopamine units.

A Powerful but Dangerous High

Users have described the meth high as the best feeling they have ever experienced and could ever imagine. Richard Lovette, a meth addict for years, describes the first moments of the high in this way, "It's like wheeeooo! And I just sit back. Can't move. Everything I have in my mind just goes. My hate, my anger, my frustrations, gone. It's pure love."[1]

As with most stimulant drugs, as time progresses the addict has to take higher and higher doses in order to gain the euphoric high. With repeated use the dopamine receptors in the brain become damaged. Eventually, methamphetamine actually reconfigures brain chemistry, destroying the emotion and pleasure centers. Addicts then require the drug simply

> " Methamphetamine actually reconfigures brain chemistry, destroying the emotion and pleasure centers. "

to feel any normal pleasure at all. One teenage former user describes the feeling like this:

> The first time, the drug gives you everything you lack. Quiet people talk. The talkative people aren't so annoying. But it's only the first time that it's like that. Then it all goes downhill. You lose everything but thinking of ways to find the drug. And you never get as high as you got that first time. Soon, the drug is only taking you back to normal, and you have to start living on it to be normal.[2]

Methamphetamine is a particularly beguiling illegal drug because unlike using heroin or cocaine, a meth addict can get high for days for a relatively inexpensive price. One hit of meth may cost as little as twelve dollars, though the price can increase up to eighty dollars if the national supply is slim. The high lasts an incredible eight to twenty-four hours. For comparison, the cocaine and heroin highs last only twenty to thirty minutes.

Methamphetamine Use Damages the Body

The damage to the body caused by methamphetamine is almost entirely due to the pressure the drug places on the central nervous system and blood vessels. Like all stimulant drugs, legal or illegal, methamphetamine speeds up the body's systems. It enables users to stay awake for days at a time and display unnatural strength and energy but also places great strain on the heart, arteries, and liver. Meth addicts often suffer heart attacks and strokes as well as convulsions, hypothermia, and organ damage.

Methamphetamine also causes more external damage to the body than other illegal drugs, due to damage to the blood vessels and, hence, to the skin's collagen. With the natural elasticity of the skin destroyed, many regular meth users look decades older than they are. Damage to salivary glands and oral tissue causes holes in the gums and an entire mouthful of rotted teeth. Meth users are often thin to the point of gauntness, since the drug both speeds up metabolism and kills the appetite—a reason many women cite for taking the drug.

Treatment and Rehabilitation

Addiction to methamphetamine functions similarly to addiction to other stimulants such as cocaine or PCP. Users start out getting a high from the drug as the brain releases huge amounts of dopamine in response to the drug's chemicals. Soon though, the brain adjusts and begins requiring the chemical simply to maintain its normal equilibrium. The addict must take larger and more frequent doses of the drug just to avoid the deep depression and pain that comes with a crash. Coming down off the drug often brings with it crushing depression, paranoia, and hallucinations. One former addict says, "The world was black and dark and I was totally depressed."[3]

Most experts recommend that meth addicts receive the same type of treatment as addicts of similar drugs over the long term. Identifying the drug use triggers is typically helpful. With the help of counselors, addicts consider what situations will spur them to use and then learn strategies to help them avoid those situations. Many addicts are encouraged to remove themselves from drug-filled environments, move away from their old homes and friends, and find new ones. In addition, traditional talk therapy and counseling are helpful for addicts wanting to know why they started using in the first place. Support groups, treatments that offer therapy for the entire family, and halfway houses have all proven successful in helping prevent relapses of meth use. The relapse rate for meth is similar to that of cocaine: Forty percent of addicts will use again within a year.

In the short term, however, people coming down off meth highs do need specialized treatment. For instance, antipsychotic medication can bring relief from hallucinations and paranoia and help users avoid harming themselves or others. Also, due to the stimulant properties of meth, many addicts will enter treatment centers not having eaten or slept for days or, in extreme cases, an entire month. A safe, encouraging environment in which to eat and sleep are important in the early stages of meth addiction treatment.

> " Coming down off the drug often brings with it crushing depression, paranoia, and hallucinations. "

Producing Meth

Controlling the production of methamphetamine is key to preventing its spread; however, unlike other stimulant drugs, meth can be made

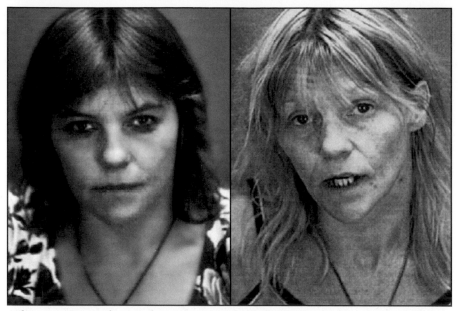

This woman, who is thirty-six in the left photograph, is pictured four years later in another police booking photograph. Once addicted to methamphetamine most find it difficult, if not impossible to stop using, causing major, irreversible damage to their bodies.

in small areas just about anywhere, making it difficult to curb the production. The drug is "cooked" in enclosed containers called "labs" in which a key ingredient—usually pseudoephedrine—is combined with other ingredients and then stewed over high temperatures. The setups in which the drug is made range from small-scale operations in private homes, remote cabins, trailers, or even the backs of vehicles such as vans, to large-scale "superlabs" in warehouses or abandoned homes. Meth labs are extremely dangerous. Explosions and chemical spills are common. The labs are also dirty—one pound of methamphetamine produces five pounds of toxic waste. The cooks manning the labs are sometimes high on the drug themselves, paranoid, and violent.

Meth labs have typically been found in both rural and suburban settings, usually in some sort of shelter with a modicum of privacy. Cooks need a certain amount of space to set up their apparatus and ingredients, though electricity is not necessary. The drug can be cooked using propane stoves and Bunsen burners. Since the spread of methamphetamine through the midwestern states in the 1990s, the majority of small-scale meth labs have been located in isolated rural areas in these states, such as house trailers or hunting cabins. The smelly fumes and potential fires of meth manufacture are easier to conceal in an out-of-the-way spot.

Some labs, however, have also been found in suburban private homes in all of the states where meth use is common. Media stories about unsuspecting residents moving into houses where meth used to be made and coming down with mysterious ailments have been rife in recent years. Claims that meth cooking will infuse the entire house with toxic chemicals that then seep into paint, carpet, and pipes and cause illness are scientifically unconfirmed, but anecdotal evidence is widespread. As of 2006 ten states had passed disclosure laws requiring that sellers tell buyers if the home was a former meth lab.

> " As of 2006 ten states had passed disclosure laws requiring that sellers tell buyers if the home was a former meth lab. "

In suburban Seattle a private citizen began an activist group after living next door to a house in which meth was being made. She was surprised at how difficult it was for police to shut the house down. The law requires police to gather large amounts of evidence just to enter a suspected meth house. She now runs an organization that teaches the public how to identify meth houses and supports police efforts trying to close them down.

Unlike large cities that are accustomed to heavy drug use, such as Philadelphia, Boston, or Washington, D.C., many areas hardest hit by meth are the least equipped to deal with the consequences of its manufacture. Once located, the meth labs must be evaluated and dismantled by trained biohazard teams. This type of work is dangerous and expensive. The state of Oklahoma, for instance, estimates the cost of cleaning up a typical meth lab to be $350,000, including the training of police officers, treatment for the users, child welfare services, and decontamination of the lab site.

Police officers in quiet midwestern towns where suburban meth labs are found are often not experienced in the violent crime that often accompanies the investigation of meth labs. Rangers and conservation officers who patrol natural areas where rural meth labs are found are equally at a disadvantage. Many officers have stated that meth has changed their jobs. One officer told *Outdoor Life* magazine, "Drug crimes have come to the forest in a big way . . . sometimes forty percent of our job is associated with drugs. . . . [Since 2001], being a forest ranger has changed one hundred and eighty degrees, and it's all due to that drug."[4]

Public Education and Government Intervention

Existing nonprofit organizations such as the Partnership for a Drug-Free America have begun anti-meth media campaigns aimed at teenagers and young adults with catchy slogans and graphic images. New groups dedicated exclusively to fighting the drug have cropped up as methamphetamine has moved to the forefront of the nation's consciousness. In Montana a software executive dedicated $5.6 million of his own fortune to create the Montana Meth Project, which creates hip, gruesome, public service announcements to discourage users from trying meth.

Other meth-prevention efforts in hard-hit states have been at the governmental level. One way the extent of methamphetamine's presence in a state can be gauged is by the corresponding severity of the state's laws addressing the drug and its manufacture. Oregon and Washington have some of the nation's most stringent meth laws; they have also been the most heavily affected for the longest period of time. In comparison, at the time of this writing, Massachusetts and other New England states had just begun considering laws aimed specifically at methamphetamine control, though those states are as yet unaffected.

> In Oregon all cold medicine with [pseudoephedrine] is available by prescription only.

Controlling the supply of ephedrine and pseudoephedrine has been at the heart of much of the state legislation. As of 2006 more than thirty-five states had placed limits on the amount of cold medicine containing pseudoephedrine a consumer could buy at one time. Similar measures include putting the drugs behind a counter or in a locked case, requiring customers wishing to purchase them to sign a log book. In Oregon all cold medicine with the chemical is available by prescription only.

Federal Efforts to Prevent Methamphetamine Use

Though the White House still names marijuana use as the nation's number one drug problem, both President George W. Bush and Congress have addressed meth addiction and prevention through legislation and funding. Increasingly, large-scale national strategies have begun flowing from the executive and legislative offices in Washington. In 2004 the Office of National Drug Control Policy released the National Synthetic Drug Action Plan, which made recommendations for the treatment, education, and regulation of methamphetamine as well as other synthetic drugs such as ecstasy. In 2006 the president signed the Combat Methamphetamine Epidemic Act, passed by Congress in 2005. The act specifically focused on controlling the flow of ephedrine and pseudoephedrine around the world, as well as supported state-level retail restrictions. The bill places sanctions on countries in which suspected meth traffickers operate. It also holds responsible foreign manufacturers of ephedrine and pseudoephedrine if their products are used to make meth. The president emphasized methamphetamine control in his annual

> " The superlabs that supply meth for the United States exist almost exclusively in Mexico. "

National Drug Control Strategy, which contained many provisions specifically aimed at curbing methamphetamine abuse, such as seizing superlabs and monitoring the flow of chemicals back and forth across the border with Mexico.

The superlabs that supply meth for the United States exist almost exclusively in Mexico, where drug control is much more lax. These massive setups are capable of producing up to ten thousand hits of meth in a single cooking session. From start to finish, the process takes about forty-eight hours and is quite profitable: Ingredients that cost under one thousand dollars can make twenty thousand dollars worth of meth.

Investigations found that certain countries, including Mexico, were importing two or three times as much raw pseudoephedrine as needed for medicine. The chemical would be processed in the Mexican superlabs and flow from there across the border into the United States. In addition, despite state efforts to regulate consumer purchase of cold medicines, pharmacies in Tijuana, Mexico, yards from the California border, would sell unlimited packs of Sudafed and Benadryl to anyone who asked.

Monitoring the International Flow

The international community has recognized the need to monitor the flow of both raw ingredients and the finished drug. In March 2006 the president of the International Narcotics Control Board, an independent Vienna-based agency, told the media, "If I want to pick on one major drug problem pandemic today, it is methamphetamine. It has not yet affected that much of western European countries and the United Kingdom but, as we know, as drug misuse occurs in North America sooner or later it gets here."[5] The board's 2005 annual report stated the need to track countries' import and export of pseudoephedrine and ephedrine and match those numbers against their legitimate demand for cold medicines in order to locate meth traffickers. The United States has called as well for the implementation of a surveillance system to provide intelligence on international meth traffickers and manufacturers.

The global nature of methamphetamine has made it a concern even for countries without a high rate of abuse. The drug's tendency to spread rapidly and its highly addictive qualities mean no region is immune. International cooperation and national awareness are essential to prevent the spread of methamphetamine addiction.

Is There a Methamphetamine Epidemic Today?

66 Meth is the No. 1 drug threat to rural America, and in many places the drug is the No. 1 threat—period. **99**

—Rusty Payne, Drug Enforcement Administration spokesman, "Methamphetamine," *CQ Researcher*, July 15, 2005.

N o consensus has been reached on whether or not the methamphetamine problem in America is truly of epidemic proportions. Scientists, public health experts, and government officials have argued convincingly for both sides. No one denies that methamphetamine use has soared in recent years. Some insist, however, that the meth problem has been exaggerated.

A Serious Problem

Many federal and state officials have issued strong statements about the extent of the meth problem. In 2004 the White House Office of National Drug Control Policy called methamphetamine "the most widely used and clandestinely produced synthetic drug in the United States."[6] In March 2006 U.S. attorney general Alberto Gonzales told a gathering of business leaders that methamphetamine is "a drug that is destroying lives and causing collateral damage in our communities."[7]

Many argue that compared with other illegal drugs, meth is associated with a much higher rate of drug-related crime and other hazards. People high on meth are frequently hyperaggressive and paranoid, making them more likely to commit violent acts. Addicts often commit both violent and petty crimes to fund their drug habit. Unlike cocaine or heroin, methamphetamine is manufactured in a process that requires open flames and high temperatures. The chemicals used to make the drug are toxic and frequently produce fumes and explosions. To compound the danger, methamphetamine is commonly manufactured in enclosed shelters such as cabins, trailers, or private homes, which can easily catch fire. All of these factors combine to create highly dangerous situations. In fact, some officials believe that methamphetamine "is perhaps the most destructive drug ever encountered," as Illinois attorney general Lisa Madigan stated in 2006.[8]

> **Police have reported that anywhere from 75 to 100 percent of those in jail were there for methamphetamine-related crimes.**

Areas of the country where methamphetamine use is widespread have experienced a steep upturn in meth-related crime and incarceration. In a 2005 survey of various law enforcement professionals, 58 percent said that methamphetamine was their biggest drug problem, compared with only 19 percent for cocaine and 3 percent for heroin. In some areas of the upper Midwest, for example, police have reported that anywhere from 75 to 100 percent of those in jail were there for methamphetamine-related crimes, prompting Montana state representative Brady Wiseman to tell *State Legislatures* magazine that methamphetamine "is now clearly a nationwide epidemic and anyone who thinks it isn't hasn't studied the issue."[9]

The Problem Is Exaggerated

Other public officials and health experts believe that the methamphetamine problem has been overstated. For instance, while the federal government has passed legislation meant to control the spread of methamphetamine, the White House Office of National Drug Control Policy still considers marijuana its main drug control concern. Methamphetamine still lags far behind the nation's most popular illegal drugs, marijuana and cocaine, which have 25 million and 6 million regular users, respectively. Part of this lag may be due to meth's relative newness on the illegal drug scene. Cocaine has been used since the nineteenth century and marijuana long before that, while meth in its present form has been around only since the 1970s.

Nonetheless, many accuse the media of contributing to a general meth hysteria, echoing the fear that surrounded the "crack craze" of the 1980s. Meth in America is merely a problem, not a "crisis," some individuals believe. In September 2005 journalist Chad Graham wrote in the *Advocate* magazine,

> It's clear that the media are hooked on meth in 2005. The volume of newspaper, magazine, and television features on the "poor man's cocaine" reeks of the hyped coverage given to inner-city crack problems in the 1980s or the terror over marijuana that swept the United States during the 1930s. Readers are awash in articles about users' rotting teeth and villages in the Midwest being destroyed by meth."[10]

Doctors have also warned the media against highlighting the more sensational aspects of meth addiction. In August 2005 a group of ninety researchers and physicians signed and published an open letter requesting that media outlets cease using the term "meth baby" to describe babies born with the drug in their bloodstreams. The label stigmatizes children and serves no useful purpose, the letter stated. The media have been guilty of covering methamphetamine stories with the intent of shocking readers rather than disseminating useful information, they wrote.

> " The White House Office of National Drug Control Policy still considers marijuana its main drug control concern. "

A National Problem

In part, officials and the media have disagreed about the scope of the methamphetamine problem in America because the drug has truly decimated certain geographic regions and heavily impacted certain demographic groups while barely affecting others. The drug has primarily affected lower-income whites in rural and semirural areas of northwestern, western, midwestern, and, more recently, southern states. Within that group more women than men are users. Those same groups on the East Coast and in New England have barely been touched at all by meth. Since the drug has not yet reached Washington, D.C., or the surrounding areas, the federal government may not fully realize the scope of the issue.

The gay communities of California and New York City have also been heavily impacted by meth use. The drug's presence in New York City in particular is notable since, for the most part, other East Coast cities, such as Philadelphia or Boston, have not been impacted. The strong cultural connection and constant flow of people to and from the West Coast cities to New York may explain meth's presence there. Lower-income whites tend to use the powdered form of meth, but the purer rock form of the drug—crystal meth—has become very popular with the gay club and party scene in Los Angeles, San Francisco, and New York City.

The West Coast states, especially Oregon and Washington, still rank as some of the states hardest hit by meth, though other western and southwestern states such as Utah, Wyoming, and Arizona have reported increases in numbers of meth users equaling those of the West Coast states. In 2004, for instance, the city of Spokane, Washington, reported that 32 percent of all men arrested tested positive for meth. Salt Lake City reported 25 percent; Phoenix, 38 percent. Not all western and southwestern states have these numbers though—San Antonio, Texas, reported only 3.5 percent. States on the East Coast did not even collect data.

> **At least a few meth labs have been uncovered in all fifty states.**

At least a few meth labs have been uncovered in all fifty states. In a 2005 study conducted by *Newsweek* magazine, certain cities in regions all across the country reported more than a 100 percent increase in emergency room visits associated with methamphetamine since 1995. Miami, for instance, cited a 233 percent increase, New Orleans, a 570 percent increase; and Atlanta, a 261 percent increase from their previously low levels.

At the time of this writing, the problem was actively spreading—both to states further east and to larger cities. In those areas that have been impacted, methamphetamine has proven itself unique in the speed with which it has swept from state to state and infiltrated communities. The current form of the drug originated on the West Coast where it was distributed by motorcycle gangs. Since then it has moved in a distinct wave from west to east across the country, advancing about five hundred miles per year, according to Richard Rawson, a UCLA neuropsychiatrist who studies the drug.

For the most part, however, methamphetamine has had the greatest impact on the rural, economically strained areas of the western half of the country where it has existed the longest. In sparsely populated counties with limited resources, the drug's impact is felt through all levels of a community, from law enforcement and courts to neglected, endangered children. In some communities, such as Anoka County in Minnesota, some 75 to 80 percent of child welfare cases are meth related, as children are removed from homes in which meth is being actively cooked or used. One social worker in the county stated, "a lot of our neglect cases have been caused because of mothers and fathers who have become addicted to meth and the kids, [who] are not getting to school, have to care for themselves."[11]

A Variety of Users

As with most illegal drugs, there is no clear-cut profile of a typical meth user. Addiction has been tracked in people of both sexes and various social classes, income levels, and ethnic backgrounds. For the most part, however, studies have shown that lower-income whites living in rural and semirural areas are by far the largest group of methamphetamine addicts. Within that group, two smaller groups have been identified as "typical" meth users: those who need to stay awake and alert, such as truckers or nightshift workers, and women, who often begin

> " There is no clear-cut profile of a typical meth user. "

taking the drug for its weight-loss effects. Because it is frequently manufactured in the home, meth tends to spread among family members. Law enforcement officials have stated that it is not uncommon to find three generations of meth addicts in one family: grandparents, parents, and adult children or teenagers.

Researchers, however, have also documented other groups who are frequent methamphetamine users. Gay men in San Francisco, San Diego, and Los Angeles began experimenting with the more expensive and purer rock form of the drug in the 1990s. Since then it has become the drug of choice for all-night partying in gay clubs. In 2003 Yves-Michel Fontaine of the Gay Men's Health Crisis told *San Francisco Gate* magazine that "we are seeing more cases of crystal meth use than in the past. We're definitely concerned about it, as are the gay men who are coming in for counseling."[12] The drug has swept through—and some feel it has decimated—certain gay enclaves with widespread crystal addiction.

Use in Europe

Methamphetamine has also spread to Europe and the United Kingdom, although this is a very recent phenomenon. In June 2006 the British government announced the drug will be listed as a "Class A" substance—an illegal drug with the highest penalty for use. This enables police to target meth labs and addicts separately from other drug investigations. A detective who pushed for this change told the *Guardian* newspaper in Manchester that "meth is arguably as much of a hazard as crack cocaine and heroin, and more of a hazard than ecstasy and LSD."[13]

The future of meth in America is uncertain. For the most part, it has yet to take hold in major East Coast cities. The *New York Times*'s Joyce Purnick suggests that the entrenchment of cocaine in these cities, which supplies the demand for illegal stimulant drugs, may be a primary reason.

This situation could soon change, however, Purnick writes, as more states restrict the sale of pseudoephedrine, meth's key ingredient. As supplies become harder to get, more may come from Mexico, which has an abundant supply and where dealers have well-established contacts in East Coast cities through the cocaine and heroin networks. Flowing methamphetamine through these channels would be an easy switch.

Evaluating the depth and scope of the methamphetamine problem in the United States has largely depended on the geographic and demographic location of the evaluator. Politicians, community leaders, and public health workers in the Northwest, Southwest, and western states have seen the devastation meth is capable of wreaking. But these problems can seem far from Congress and the White House in Washington, surrounded by East Coast cities where meth addiction is an anomaly rather than a norm. Whether methamphetamine is truly an "epidemic" in an academic sense is still under debate. Few deny, however, that the drug is a significant problem.

Is There a Methamphetamine Epidemic Today?

❝Epidemic. That's certainly an accurate way to define what's been infiltrating communities across the country in the form of a highly addictive drug called methamphetamine.❞

> —Chuck Grassley, "Wake Up to a National Epidemic," News, August 8, 2005. http://grassley.senate.gov.

Chuck Grassley is a Republican senator from Iowa.

❝[In] the United States, moral panics are most reliably directed at illicit drug users . . . For the last year, a moral panic about methamphetamine and its users has been gathering force.❞

> —Jack Shafer, "Meth Mouth, Our Latest Moral Panic," *Slate*, August 9, 2005.

Jack Shafer is editor at large for the online magazine *Slate*.

❝Media coverage of meth has distorted the scale of its use, hyping it as a national story while creating concern about problems in regions where none exist.❞

> —Ryan S. King, "Meth Epidemic Just Media Hype," *Arizona Republic*, June 25, 2006.

Ryan S. King is a policy analyst with the Sentencing Project, a nonprofit prisoners' rights organization.

* Editor's Note: While the definition of a primary source can be narrowly or broadly defined, for the purposes of Compact Research, a primary source consists of: 1) results of original research presented by an organization or researcher; 2) eyewitness accounts of events, personal experience, or work experience; 3) first-person editorials offering pundits' opinions; 4) government officials presenting political plans and/or policies; 5) representatives of organizations presenting testimony or policy.

66We've been reluctant to respond to the tinny little chorus of media critics and drug-control skeptics who claim this newspaper and others have cooked up the nation's methamphetamine problem . . . it's hard to argue with anyone who can look seriously . . . at meth use and addiction . . . and still insist that the problem is a 'myth.'**99**

—*Portland Oregonian*, "In the Fight Against Meth, No Apologies Are Necessary," July 16, 2006.

The *Oregonian* newspaper, based in Portland, Oregon, is responsible for award-winning coverage of methamphetamine abuse by reporter Steve Suo and others.

66Methamphetamine has taken on the role once played by heroin, and later by crack, in the public imagination—a drug so deeply destructive and addictive that there is no chance of release from its grip.**99**

—Patrick Moore, "Tweaking the Crystal Meth Myth," *Los Angeles Times*, June 11, 2006.

Patrick Moore is a former meth addict and author of *Tweaked: A Crystal Meth Memoir*.

66We are deeply disappointed that American and international media as well as some policy makers continue to use stigmatizing terms and unfounded assumptions [when discussing methamphetamine addiction] that . . . lack any scientific basis.**99**

—Join Together, "Meth Science Not Stigma: An Open Letter to the Media," July 27, 2005. www.jointogether.org.

Ninety-two signatories, mostly researchers, physicians, and public health officials, signed the open letter published on the Web site for the drug treatment and prevention organization Join Together.

66 [Use] and production of methamphetamine . . . has had an especially severe impact in the Midwest, Northwest, and certain areas of the South.99

— Bertha Madras, testimony before the House Committee on Government Reform, June 28, 2006.

Bertha Madras is a deputy director with the White House's Office of National Drug Control Policy.

66 Athletes and students sometimes begin using meth because of the initial heightened physical and mental performance. . . . Blue collar and service workers may use the drug to work extra shifts, while young women often begin using the drug to lose weight.99

—KCI: The Anti-Meth Site, 2006. www.kci.org.

KCI is a nonprofit organization that seeks to educate the public about methamphetamine addiction through its informational Web site.

66 Meth is the drug of ordinary Americans. Housewives use it to get through the day, truck drivers to endure long, lonely journeys.99

—Ki-Min Sung, "It's 'Pleasantville' with Dementia, Impotence and Rotten Teeth," *Los Angeles Times*, July 9, 2006.

Ki-Min Sung is an arts and lifestyle reporter for the *Dallas Morning News*.

66 [Meth] has a different impact than any other kind of drug because of this multiplicity of effect: of endangerment to fire departments, endangerment to the policemen, endangerment to children.99

—Mark Souder, "The Meth Epidemic," *Frontline*, transcribed interview, PBS, February 14, 2006. www.pbs.org.

Mark Souder is a Republican representative from Indiana, a state heavily affected by methamphetamine. He helped create the federal Combat Methamphetamine Epidemic Act of 2005.

❝[There] has been a substantial increase in the illicit use of methylamphetamine in the Far East, parts of Europe and North America . . . but, so far, there has been relatively little evidence of misuse in the UK.❞

—Michael Rawlins, "Methylamphetamine," letter to home secretary, June 5, 2006. www.drugs.gov.uk.

Michael Rawlins is the chair of the Advisory Council on the Misuse of Drugs, a division of the Home Office in the United Kingdom.

❝If I want to pick on one major drug problem pandemic today, it is methamphetamine.❞

—Hamid Ghodse, "Lax Laws 'Could Turn Nazi Crank into Global Epidemic,'" *Times* (London), March 1, 2006.

Hamid Ghodse is the president of the International Narcotics Control Board, a United Nations drug control administration.

Is There a Methamphetamine Epidemic Today?

- In a 2005 survey of various law enforcement professionals by the National Association of Counties, 58 percent said that methamphetamine was their biggest drug problem, as compared with only 19 percent for cocaine and only 3 percent for heroin.

- In some areas of the Upper Midwest, police reported that anywhere from 75 to 100 percent of those in jail were there for methamphetamine-related crimes, according to the National Association of Counties.

- Many women report that they first started using methamphetamine to lose weight.

- Meth use first became popular on the West Coast but has since spread to the western and midwestern states.

- Meth can be manufactured in a variety of locations, but labs are most often found in isolated rural or semirural areas.

- According to the *New York Times*, up to 77 percent of meth users are white, as opposed to only 4 percent African American.

- In the 2004 National Survey on Drug Use and Health, more men than women reported having tried meth in their lifetimes.

- *Newsweek* magazine reports that in 2003, 12.3 million Americans have reported trying meth at least once, up 40 percent from 2000.

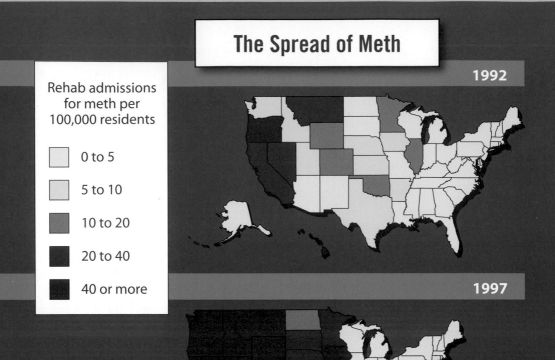

The Spread of Meth

1992

Rehab admissions for meth per 100,000 residents

- 0 to 5
- 5 to 10
- 10 to 20
- 20 to 40
- 40 or more

1997

2002

These maps show how methamphetamine spread across the country between 1992 and 2002. The spread was measured by the number of people seeking help in rehab centers.

Source: Derrik Quenzer and Steve Suo, "The Spread of Meth." *The Oregonian*, www.oregonlive.com.

Number of Persons over Age 12 Who First Used Specific Substances in the Prior Year

This chart tracks the number of people over the age of twelve who first began using certain illegal drugs during a certain year. From 1992 to 2003, the number of new meth users increased by 68 percent. New meth use surpassed new crack use for the first time in 2003.

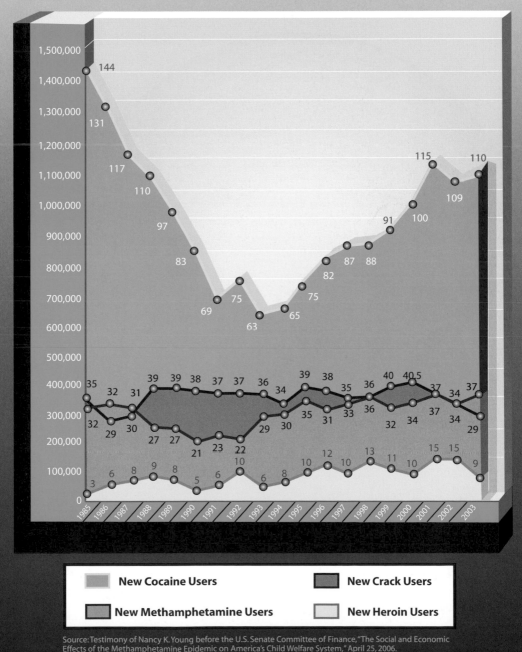

New Cocaine Users   New Crack Users

New Methamphetamine Users   New Heroin Users

Source: Testimony of Nancy K. Young before the U.S. Senate Committee of Finance, "The Social and Economic Effects of the Methamphetamine Epidemic on America's Child Welfare System," April 25, 2006.

33

Meth Use in Past Year Among Persons Aged 12 or Older, by Race/Ethnicity, 2002–2004

This graph outlines the race or ethnicity of methamphetamine users over a three-year period. Native Hawaiians have a disproportionately large percentage due to the drug's prevalence in Hawaii and other Pacific islands. Meth's presence on American Indian reservations is also apparent in the numbers of Native Americans represented. Asians, African Americans, and Latinos trail whites in meth use.

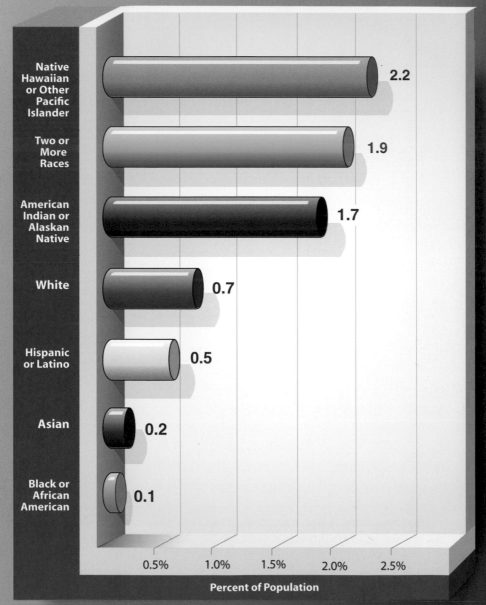

Race/Ethnicity	Percent of Population
Native Hawaiian or Other Pacific Islander	2.2
Two or More Races	1.9
American Indian or Alaskan Native	1.7
White	0.7
Hispanic or Latino	0.5
Asian	0.2
Black or African American	0.1

Percent of Population

Source: Testimony of Nancy K. Young before the U.S. Senate Committee on Finance, "The Social and Economic Effects of the Methamphetamine Epidemic on America's Child Welfare System," April 25, 2006.

- The addiction rate for methamphetamine is similar to that of cocaine.

- The National Institute on Drug Abuse found in a 2004 survey that 6.2 percent of high school students reported that they had used meth at least once, the same percentage as in 2003.

Meth Use Ahead of Cocaine and Heroin

The following chart shows the percentage of people who have used specific illicit drugs sometime in their lives. Marijuana is by far the most common drug used, with over 40 percent of all people having tried the drug at least once. About 5 percent of people have tried meth, more than have used powder cocaine and heroin but far less than those who have tried crack cocaine, which had over 14 percent.

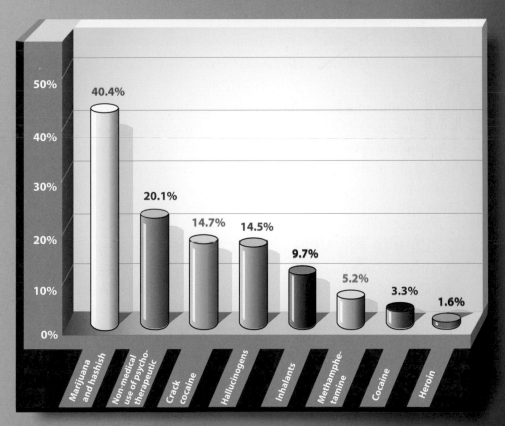

Source: National Survey on Drug Use and Health, "Illicit Drug Use in Lifetime (Among Persons Age 12 and Over)," Substance Abuse and Mental Health Services Administration, 2003.

How Dangerous Is Methamphetamine Use?

> 66 [She] was brought home at 3 a.m. on January 3, 2004, strung out on meth. . . . We took her to the emergency room where they hooked her up to IVs to slow down her heart rate. At this point, my husband and I felt as if we were losing our daughter and wondered how much longer she would survive. 99
>
> – Moira Knutson, "My Daughter and Meth," Partnership for a Drug-Free America, August 8, 2005. www.drug freeamerica.org.

Methamphetamine is an extremely dangerous stimulant drug. It has significant adverse short-term and long-term consequences on both the mind and the body. Use of the drug also contributes to dangerous life decisions and accidents. In particular, methamphetamine abuse is the cause of many instances of unprotected sex and sexually transmitted disease (STD) and HIV transmission as well as birth defects, explosions, and fires.

Damage to Physical Appearance

More so than other illegal drugs, methamphetamine is striking in the havoc it wreaks on a user's physical appearance, even with short-term use. Most of the damage meth does is due to general damage to the body's circulatory system. It constricts blood vessels, depriving many of the body's tissues of their blood supply and causing permanent damage, as well as damaging arteries and organs. Meth addicts often look years older than their age because of damage to the blood vessels in the skin. The result of this damage is that the skin wrinkles and hangs in folds. Methamphetamine also causes extreme weight loss because it both speeds up the metabolism and kills the appetite. In addition, users often forget to eat when high. They tend to appear gaunt and emaciated, adding to their prematurely aged look.

"Meth mouth" is a physical effect unique to methamphetamine and one that is particularly disturbing to see. Most users grind their teeth repeatedly because of the increased anxiety caused by the drug. Grinding wears down the enamel and causes extensive cavities. The drug dries out the salivary glands, causing the mouth's acids to eat away at the teeth and gums. Meth also damages the mouth itself, hastening gum decay. All of these effects combine to cause an entire mouthful of rotten teeth and holes in gums, tongue, and cheeks. The damage is truly extensive. "Some users describe their teeth as 'blackened, stained, rotting, crumbling or falling apart,'"[14] stated oral surgeon Robert M. Brandjord in a January 2006 statement during a national methamphetamine conference. Meth users tend to lose most or all of their teeth, even at a very young age.

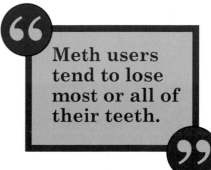

Meth users tend to lose most or all of their teeth.

One of the most obvious physical signs of a regular meth user, aside from a gaunt frame and rotted teeth, are telltale open sores and welts scattered over the arms and face, especially near the lips. Because blood vessels are damaged, wounds do not heal well and often become infected. These sores are the result of a common meth hallucination brought on by the drug's effects on the nerves, in which users imagine that insects are crawling under or on their skin. This hallucination is called *formication* and is sometimes seen with other synthetic drugs, such as LSD or PCP. As a result, users pick and scratch at their skin repeatedly until sores form, often becoming oozing welts.

Meth Causes Brain Damage

In addition to widespread damage to blood vessels, scientists have found evidence of permanent emotional and cognitive damage in longtime meth users. A psychology professor at the University of Southern California reports that methamphetamine, if used heavily, actually shrinks the brain up to 1 percent a year. The drug's destruction of the dopamine receptors in the brain makes it difficult for many meth addicts to feel normal pleasure in ordinary activities such as eating or sex. The receptors can grow back; however, some former meth addicts who have been clean for years report still being unable to feel any sort of pleasure. Over the long term, users can develop a motor disorder similar to Parkinson's disease from the damage to their brain cells, in addition to severe memory and coordination problems.

A body during an actual meth high is under a great deal of strain. The drug speeds up all of the body's systems, increasing metabolism and heart rate and straining the central nervous and circulatory systems. This strain greatly increases a meth user's risk of stroke, liver damage, heart attack, and convulsions. Blood vessels are unnaturally dilated. In essence, the body becomes unable to regulate its systems and maintain equilibrium.

During a high, depending on the dose, users can spike a fever up to 107 degrees. "Overheating is the primary reason for meth deaths,"[15] neuropsychiatrist Richard Rawson told the *Oregonian* newspaper. Those high on meth can also become dangerously dehydrated because the drug kills their ability to feel their natural thirst.

Bizarre, Unsafe Behavior

Another unique characteristic of methamphetamine is the length of the high and subsequent "crash." Meth users can get high for up to two days off one hit of meth—as opposed to the mere hours provided by a cocaine or heroin high. The length of the downward crash is equivalent. When coming down from the high, users frequently feel anxious, paranoid, confused, and irritable. This period, during the hours- or days-long descent from the initial burst of euphoria, is when users tend to display bizarre behavior, all stemming from the effects of the drug on the body's central nervous system. One of the most common meth-fueled behaviors is called "tweaking," in which users perform bizarre, repetitive, meaningless tasks over and over, such as washing dishes again and again, putting duct tape over windows, or plucking out body hair. Frequently, these behaviors are somehow related to the paranoia that a meth high brings, such as barricading oneself in a room. Meth addicts sometimes refer to themselves as "tweakers."

> " Meth users can get high for up to two days off one hit of meth. "

One of the most frequently cited and far-reaching consequences of methamphetamine use is high-risk sexual behavior. Along with euphoria, the drug brings on heightened sensations and hypersexual feelings. This, combined with the severely impaired judgment and recklessness typical of a meth high, has led to high numbers of meth users engaging in unprotected sex with multiple partners. This has resulted in an increase in HIV and other sexually transmitted diseases—among gay men in particular.

Impact on the Gay Community

Methamphetamine has especially affected the gay communities of San Francisco and New York City. Some estimates put the number of gay men in San Francisco who have tried crystal meth at 40 percent, which is far above the national average. Almost always, the drug is used in a party atmosphere. Meth is not expensive, it increases sexual desire, and provides stamina for all-night parties, which are common in gay clubs. *Newsweek*'s David Jefferson reports on the increasing popularity of Party and Play gatherings in the gay community. These are parties in which groups of gay men get together in hotel suites or homes specifically to smoke meth and have sex. Despite this intimacy, people high on meth often are aggressive, paranoid, and emotionally detached, creating scenes that can be either dangerous or startlingly robotic.

> " California health experts estimate that gay men who are regular meth users are twice as likely to be HIV positive as those who are not. "

Most gay men, when high on meth, do not use condoms when having sex. They snort or inject crystal and then have unprotected anal sex with multiple partners. The chance of HIV transmission is further increased by the tendency of users to assume sexual positions that leave one even more vulnerable to transferring the virus. The danger is real, says Jeffrey Klausner of the San Francisco Department of Public Health. "The crystal meth epidemic is playing an important role in increasing sexual risk behaviors, and that is leading to new HIV and STD infections."[16] California health experts estimate that gay men who are regular meth users are twice as likely to be HIV positive as those who are not.

To complicate matters, evidence has emerged that the presence of methamphetamine in the blood may somehow suppress immunity and increase the amount of HIV virus present in the blood. In February 2005, New York City officials announced that a rare, drug-resistant super strain of HIV had been detected in a man who had a long history of crystal meth use. Since then, scientists have speculated that meth's chemicals may somehow impact the body's immune cells, suppressing those that combat the virus. In addition, the damage to the blood vessels of the body, including those in the mucous membranes, may cause many more cuts and open sores, thus increasing chances of infection.

Other Serious Consequences

Some of the consequences of methamphetamine use extend beyond the body of the user. Babies born with methamphetamine in their blood tend to have a variety of problems, including low birth weight, excessive crying, attention deficit disorder, and behavior problems. A 2005 University of Toronto study found that babies whose mothers used meth even one time during pregnancy have a higher risk of birth defects, including brain damage. The babies born with meth in their blood had birth defects at a rate 4.5 times higher than babies without drugs in their blood. In contrast, babies born with crack in their bloodstreams had birth defects 1.3 more times.

> " In August 2005, *Newsweek* magazine reported that burn center admissions were up drastically in meth-affected areas of the country. "

The unique conditions under which methamphetamine is cooked add to the danger of the drug. Echoing crack cocaine's precursor, freebase, meth's raw ingredients must be combined over high temperatures, using potentially explosive chemicals such as lye, ammonia, or fertilizer. The cooking frequently takes place in private homes or trailers and by cooks either high on the drug themselves or crashing off of it. Fires and explosions are so common that in August 2005, *Newsweek* magazine reported that burn center admissions were up drastically in meth-affected areas of the country. Treating burn victims is lengthy and expensive and meth-related burns are often even more complicated than burns caused by ordinary fires because of the presence of toxic chemicals. Most meth-burn victims have no health insurance, leaving the burden of caring for them on already cash-strapped facilities.

As these accidents demonstrate, methamphetamine use creates a burden, not only on the body of the user but on the larger community. Government, medical facilities, and social services all must stretch to absorb the consequences of meth addiction. The drug's swift destruction of the body's systems and the reckless behavior brought on by the high has grave and expensive consequences.

How Dangerous Is Methamphetamine Use?

66 **Meth is an equal opportunity destroyer. I have many friends and family members whose lives have been devastated by this horrible drug. Countless grandparents across America are raising their grandchildren because their children are addicted to meth.** 99

—Rob Bovett, "Meth: The Oregon Front," Oregon Public Broadcasting, 2006. www.opb.org.

Rob Bovett is the legal counsel for the Oregon Narcotics Enforcement Association.

66 **Methamphetamine is a powerfully addictive stimulant associated with serious health conditions, including memory loss, aggression, psychotic behavior, and potential heart and brain damage; it also contributes to increased transmission of hepatitis and HIV/AIDS.** 99

—Glen R. Hanson, "Methamphetamine Abuse and Addiction," National Institute on Drug Abuse Research Report Series, January 2002.

Glen R. Hanson is the former acting director of the National Institute on Drug Abuse, part of the U.S. Department of Health and Human Services.

* Editor's Note: While the definition of a primary source can be narrowly or broadly defined, for the purposes of Compact Research, a primary source consists of: 1) results of original research presented by an organization or researcher; 2) eyewitness accounts of events, personal experience, or work experience; 3) first-person editorials offering pundits' opinions; 4) government officials presenting political plans and/or policies; 5) representatives of organizations presenting testimony or policy.

66 Meth mouth is characterized by rampant [cavities] or tooth decay. . . often there is no hope of treating methamphetamine-damaged teeth, leading to full mouth [tooth] extractions. 99

—Robert M. Brandjord, statement of the American Dental Association at the National Town Hall on Methamphetamine Awareness and Prevention, January 23, 2006.

Robert M. Brandjord is an oral surgeon and president of the American Dental Association.

66 Before I started [using methamphetamine], I was a pretty cute girl and then I thought I broke out, so I treated it like you would acne. Come to find out . . . those were 'tweaker sores.' I still get them even after I quit. 99

—"Rainylove," "Methamphetamine: Stories and Letters of the Hidden Costs," KCI: The Anti-Meth Site, 2006. www.kci.org.

This quote is a testimonial posted on an anti-meth site by a former addict.

66 When she was high . . . she had to be on the computer— diddling with the programs to make them run faster, ordering freebies on the Internet. . . . Then computers faded and she was obsessed with diving into dumpsters. . . . 99

—Thea Singer, "Recipe for Disaster," *Washington Post*, January 15, 2006.

Thea Singer is a freelance journalist and sister of a former methamphetamine addict.

66 When you're on meth you have the most energy in the world. You're organizing stupid things, like your sock drawer, over and over again. You have this feeling of total power and ability. 99

—Ruth Andrew Ellenson, "The Amount of Lying and Covering Up Was Insane," *People*, February 20, 2006.

This quote is from an interview with Jodie Sweeten, a television actor who was formerly addicted to crystal methamphetamine. As a child, she appeared on the popular series *Full House*.

❝My dance with meth began in my late teens. I fell in love with a man. [The] closest that I could get to [the feelings I experienced with him] were the feelings of euphoria and power that I found when I was tweaking.❞

—Robbie M., "Enslaved and Released," Tweaker.org, 2004. www.tweaker.org.

Robbie M. is a gay former crystal meth addict who describes his addiction on the Web site Tweaker.org.

❝If there is but one message to take home . . . it is this: people can and do recover from methamphetamine addiction.❞

—Lewis E. Gallant, testimony submitted to Senate Appropriations Committee, Subcommittee on Labor, Health and Human Services, Education and Related Agencies, Hearing on Methamphetamine Abuse, April 21, 2005.

Lewis E. Gallant is the executive director of the National Association of State Alcohol and Drug Abuse Directors.

❝The rapidly growing use of crystal methamphetamine in New York City continues to play a significant role in facilitating the transmission of HIV.❞

—Thomas R. Frieden, statement by New York City Health Commissioner Dr. Thomas R. Frieden on Rare Strain of HIV in a New York City Resident, New York City Department of Health, February 24, 2005. www.nyc.gov.

Thomas R. Frieden is the health commissioner of New York City.

❝My boyfriend was a meth cook. . . . I was living on the doorstep of death everyday, almost unknowingly because I had no idea how toxic and explosive the chemicals used to make meth were at the time.❞

—Mindy McConnell, "I Could Never Get High Enough," Partnership for a Drug-Free America, May 9, 2006. www.drugfreeamerica.org.

Mindy McConnell is a former methamphetamine addict.

❝Volatile meth labs assembled in homes have resulted in explosions, which maim and kill not only those cooking the drug, but also their families.❞

—John D. Dingell, statement before the U.S. House Committee on Energy and Commerce to consider H.R. 3889, November 15, 2005.

John D. Dingell is a Democratic representative from Michigan who sits on the House Committee on Energy and Commerce and has pushed for methamphetamine legislation.

....

❝Meth addiction not only affects the users, but also the friends and family.❞

—Crystal Meth Anonymous, "For the Addict," 2006. www.crystalmeth.org.

Crystal Meth Anonymous is a twelve-step program for methamphetamine addicts. It has chapters across the country.

....

How Dangerous Is Methamphetamine Use?

- Mitch Earleywine, psychology professor at the University of Southern California, has reported that methamphetamine, if used heavily, actually shrinks the brain up to 1 percent a year.

- Meth increases the heart rate to the extent that many meth users report feeling as though they were going to have a heart attack while high on the drug.

- Meth users are at a higher risk for hypothermia because their blood vessels are unnaturally dilated and they are unable to regulate their body temperature.

- Crystal meth users are three times more likely to be HIV positive as nonusers.

- Meth both impairs the judgment centers in the brain and increases libido, frequently causing users to engage in risky sexual behavior.

- In 2004, 80 percent of new clients to the drug counseling program at the Gay Men's Health Crisis report meth as their main drug problem, up from fewer than half in 2001.

- In the gay community the vast majority of addicts use the rock form of the drug rather than the powdered form.

How Meth Affects the Brain

This illustration shows how meth affects the brain. The drug stimulates the brain's production and release of dopamine, a chemical in the body known to create feelings of pleasure. However, meth abuse can cause damage to the dopamine production process, making it difficult for addicts to feel pleasure when off the drug. Dopamine is manufactured in nerve cells within the ventral tegmental area of the brain then released in the nucleus accumbens and the frontal cortex.

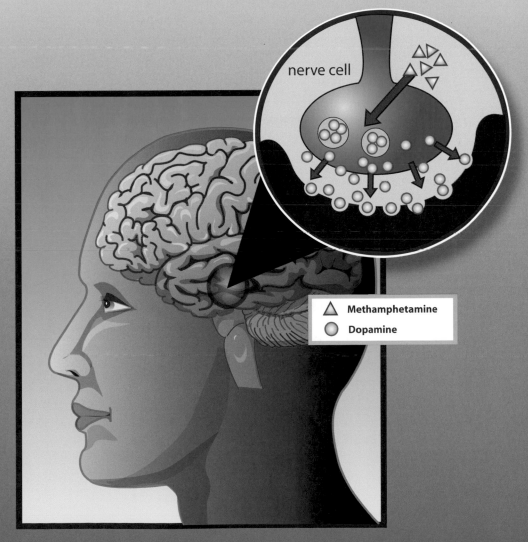

nerve cell

△ Methamphetamine

○ Dopamine

Source: NIDA Research and Report Series, *Methamphetamine Abuse and Addiction*, "What Are the Long-Term Effects of Methamphetamine Abuse?" February 4, 2005.

- A 2005 University of Toronto study found that babies whose mothers used meth even one time during pregnancy have a higher risk of birth defects, including brain damage.

- In a 2005 University of California at Davis study, one in ten babies born at the UC-Davis Medical Center had methamphetamine in their blood.

- Because of the effects on their developing brains, the fumes from methamphetamine cooking pose a special risk to children who breathe them.

How Meth Affects the Body

This table sumarizes the short- and long- term effects of meth abuse. Short-term effects include increased alertness and decreased fatigue, while long-term effects can include paranoia, stroke, and weight loss.

Short-Term Effects	Long-Term Effects
Increased attention and decreased fatigue	Dependence and addiction psychosis
Increased activity	Paranoia
Decreased appetite	Hallucinations
Euphoria and rush	Mood disturbances
Increased respiration	Repetitive motor activity
Hypothermia	Stroke
	Weight loss

Source: NIDA Research and Report Series, *Methamphetamine Abuse and Addiction*, "What Are the Long-Term Effects of Methamphetamine Abuse?" February 4, 2005.

Meth Treatment Admission Rate per 100,000 Population Aged 12 or Older, 1992–2002

This graph shows that treatment for methamphetamine use is on the rise, indicating that use, in general, is on the rise.

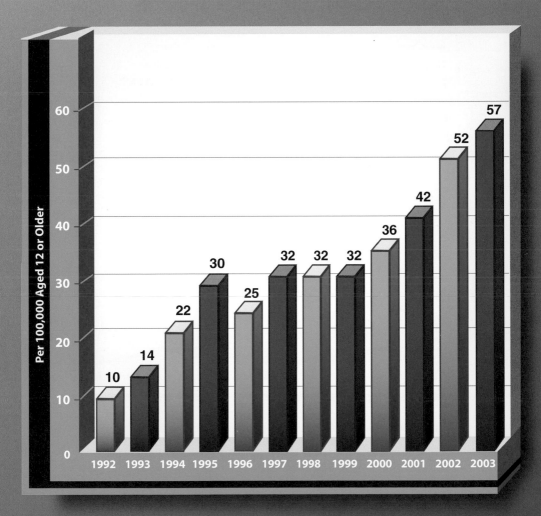

Source: 2002 SAMHSA Treatment Episode Data Set (TEDS), July 7, 2006. www.oas.samhsa.gov.

Meth Admissions by Method of Use, 1992–2002

Meth can be inhaled, smoked, injected, and taken orally. In 1992, 39 percent of primary meth treatment admissions had inhaled the drug, while 12 percent had smoked it. By 2002 only 17 percent had inhaled the drug and 50 percent had smoked it. The other methods of use remained relatively stable during the time period.

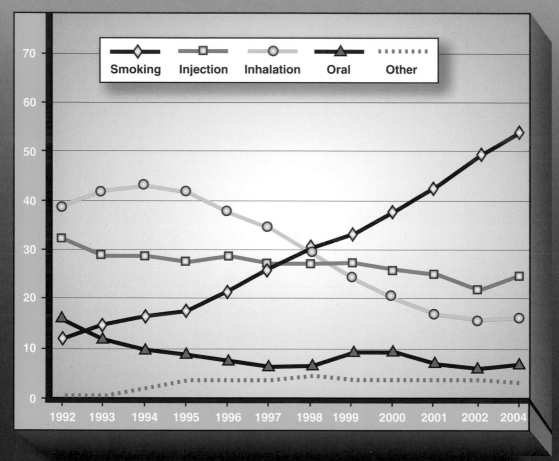

Source: 2002 SAMHSA Treatment Episode Data Set (TEDS), July 7, 2006. www.samhsa.gov.

Is There a Link Between Methamphetamine Addiction and Crime?

> **After it invades the central nervous system to achieve its high, meth turns perfectly normal people into psychotics, often violent ones.**
>
> —Andrea Neal, "Drug War: An American Epidemic," *Saturday Evening Post*, January/February 2006.

Areas of the country that have a high rate of methamphetamine addiction also tend to experience a proportional rise in both violent and nonviolent crime. This correlation is not unique to methamphetamine—areas affected heavily by crack cocaine and other drugs have had similar experiences. The phenomenon is more pronounced with meth, because for the most part, the drug has so far manifested itself mainly in rural or semirural areas.

This is not to say that methamphetamine-related crime does not exist in urban areas—it does. But much of the attention surrounding meth and crime tends to focus on suburban and rural regions. The crack cocaine problem, for instance, existed mainly in the urban centers of large cities with extensive public services and huge populations. When even a dozen people in a small midwestern town become addicted to meth, the aftereffects are instantly noticeable. In addition, unlike major cities, most of these areas have rarely experienced drug-related violent crime in the past. Police, the courts, and social services do not tend to be equipped for problems of this scale.

As meth has spread from the West Coast into the Midwest and western states, crime has followed. The increases in heavily affected areas can be striking. In Ramsey County, Minnesota, for instance, there were 24 meth-related prosecutions in 1999; in 2004 there were 301. In Texas, 50 percent of counties reported that one in five of all incarcerations were related to methamphetamine.

Meth crime tends to divide itself naturally into three categories: crimes committed in order to obtain meth, crimes committed while under the influence of meth, and child abuse or neglect by meth-addicted parents or guardians. All of these are dangerous and destructive to both the addict and his or her environment. As one teenage addict stated, "Once you start taking drugs you turn into a nasty, horrible person. . . . I treated people like crap. My only goal was to get money to get meth."[17]

Getting Money for Meth

Users trying to find money to buy meth tend to commit nonviolent crimes such as stealing, car theft, or burglary to get goods to sell or trade for the drug. Like those addicted to other drugs, such as cocaine or heroin, these are often desperate, unplanned acts. One incarcerated addict told *Esquire* magazine that "tweakers will steal anything you can imagine. Like bridges. I'm serious, they'll unbolt the metal on bridges, put it on the back of their trucks, and sell it to the metal-recycling place in the morning. Meth blocks out anything you care about. The only thing you care about is the next . . . fix."[18]

Petty crimes such as passing bad checks, forgery, and mail fraud are also common among meth users. Identity theft has been a particular problem. In 2004 *USA Today* reported on the bust of a Canadian meth smuggling ring so sophisticated that it controlled dozens of bank accounts, using documents found in dumpsters behind cell phone customer service centers. Ringleaders paid addicts with meth in return for their Internet skills, eventually stealing thousands of dollars. However, this incident, while sensational, was not typical of the average meth crime.

Coming Off a High

Methamphetamine users experience a sometimes hours- or even days-long downward slide as they come off a high. This is the period during which addicts are most likely to commit violent acts and are most dangerous to themselves and others. After the initial burst of euphoria, the drug brings on feelings of hyperaggression, anger, and paranoia, hallucinations, and recklessness. Often, users will display superhuman strength and ability to withstand pain as the drug overwhelms the pain sensors in their brains. Ordinary judgment and moral boundaries can be complete-ly obliterated. These effects are not limited only to methamphetamine. People high on PCP and LSD tend to display similar behavior.

Local media in meth-affected areas have reported extensively on these criminal acts perpetrated by addicts. The *Omaha World-Herald* in Ne-braska described a policeman chasing a carjacking suspect who was high on meth. He shot the man with both a Taser gun and pepper spray, apparently with no effect. A Drug Enforcement Ad-ministration officer in Colorado told the *Denver Post* that officers frequently find large caches of weapons in meth houses. "The meth culture is intertwined with weapons of all kinds," he stated. "We see a degree of weapons and violence with other drugs but not to the degree that we see it with meth."[19] The *Saturday Evening Post* reported that a man high on meth beheaded his fourteen-year-old son and threw the head from his van onto a busy highway.

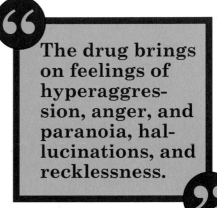

The drug brings on feelings of hyperaggres-sion, anger, and paranoia, hal-lucinations, and recklessness.

Are Stories of Meth Crime Exaggerated?

Law enforcement officers are particularly vulnerable to the paranoia and irrationality displayed by addicts coming off the high. The California at-torney general's Web site offers tips for officers encountering an addict in this state, such as avoiding the use of bright lights and loud voices since the user's senses are heightened:

> Slow your movements. This will decrease the odds the [addict] will misinterpret your physical actions. . . . Keep the [addict] talking. An [addict] who falls silent can be extremely dangerous. Silence often means that his para-noid thoughts have taken over reality and anyone present can become part of [his] paranoid delusions.[20]

Anecdotal stories about the dangers police face when discovering or shutting down meth houses are common. Houses are sometimes booby-trapped and some addicts have a tendency to stockpile weapons, according to media reports. Frequently, violence is random and based on drug-induced paranoia. One Bureau of Land Management ranger reported being shot at by teenagers high on meth who had no previous criminal records at all.

Some believe, however, that the stories of crime committed by methamphetamine addicts are exaggerated. Stories that illustrate the horrors of drug abuse sell well, these critics point out. In addition, the stories of meth-addicted criminals roaming the streets are strikingly similar to stories in the 1980s of hordes of crack addicts taking over the inner cities. A 2006 survey by the National Association of Counties (NACO) that outlined the prevalence of meth-related crime has come under particular fire. Jack Shafer of *Slate* magazine accuses NACO of conducting shoddy research that generates results the media wants. Statistics expert Maia Szalavitz also points out that it is in the interest of NACO to produce high meth-crime numbers since these surveys are directly related to the level of funding the association will receive. Most media that reported on the NACO survey "[did not] note that the survey was a lobbying document, sponsored by the group in aid of its efforts to get more funding for methamphetamine anti-drug task forces,"[21] Szalavitz writes on her Web site, Stats.org. The NACO survey has been widely accepted, however, and cited by reputable media outlets as an accurate presentation of the state of much of the nation with regard to meth.

Meth Prisons Are Controversial

One of the offshoots of the rise in meth-related crimes has been the invention of "meth prisons"—entire facilities dedicated exclusively to criminals addicted to methamphetamine. Authorities tout the prisons as a way of keeping addicts away from the active trade in meth that goes on in most ordinary facilities. The prisons also include intensive drug treatment programs and rehabilitation classes to train addicts to control their urges once they are released.

These prisons are not without controversy, however. Critics of the facilities argue that meth is seen as a "white" drug because most of its users are white. Crack users on the other hand, are more often African Americans from poor urban areas. The criticism is that crack addicts are not being housed in special facilities and offered extensive rehabilitation. Greg Mathis, a judge and African American activist writes, "[It] seems that meth users, by way of the criminal justice system, are getting the help they need to get their lives back on track while, historically, crack use has been punished with stiff criminal sentences."[22] In addition, Ryan S. King of the Sentencing Project, a nonprofit organization that advocates sentencing reform, points out that even these special facilities do not have treatment and support available after prisoners are released, increasing the chances that they will return to meth abuse.

Meth Use Leads to Child Abuse

Parents and guardians addicted to illegal drugs rarely are able to properly care for their children. Because methamphetamine's highs and lows can last for days, however, child neglect and abuse tends to be more common among addicts of that drug. Children living in homes where methamphetamine is used may bear the brunt of the aggressiveness that comes with a meth high. A parent using the drug might be affected for a week, for instance, during which time they may not eat or sleep. Coming off a high, meth users will frequently sleep for days—obviously unable to feed or care for the children in their household. In addition, because the cooking process is so toxic and meth is frequently made in the home, children are often exposed to toxic fumes, which cause lung problems, and burns from chemical spills or fires.

"One county in Minnesota reported that more than half of all child protection cases were meth related.

Child protection workers have reported an increase in their caseloads in areas with high rates of methamphetamine abuse. One county in Minnesota reported that more than half of all child protection cases were meth related. The National Association of Counties reported that in 2004, 40 percent of child welfare officials in thirteen states had increases in foster care placements directly related to parental meth abuse.

Is Meth Coverage Sensationalized?

Among social critics there is no general consensus about whether methamphetamine increases rates of crime or child abuse. For as many that are convinced that the nation is in the midst of a meth-induced crime wave, there are just as many who believe that the drug is neither more widespread nor more destructive than crack cocaine or heroin; however, these critics tend to disagree as a whole with U.S. drug policy. They consider most media coverage of illegal drugs to be hype. Methamphetamine is just the latest drug of choice for fearmongers, they argue.

There is no doubt, however, that methamphetamine abuse does lead to criminal acts. The drug may or may not be more harmful or destructive than other drugs, and reports of methamphetamine crimes may or may not be sensationalized by the media. No one denies that people who take meth are more likely to commit crimes of various sorts than those who do not. Objective analysis of crime statistics and impartial reporting, however, are essential to the continued assessment of the problem.

Is There a Link Between Methamphetamine Addiction and Crime?

66 Communities all across America are suffering from the plague of methamphetamine production and usage. And these communities . . . are looking for effective and innovative ways to fight back against this illegal menace. 99

—Meth Watch Program, "Looking Out for Our Communities." www.methwatch.com.

Meth Watch is a nonprofit organization that helps retailers monitor suspicious customer purchases that may indicate methamphetamine manufacturing.

66 One hundred percent of the methamphetamine problem is caused by one thing—addiction to meth. Without addiction there is no demand, therefore, no labs, no crime, no child abuse related to meth. 99

—Jay Wurscher, "Meth: The Oregon Front," Oregon Public Broadcasting, 2006. www.opb.org.

Jay Wurscher is the Oregon Child Welfare Alcohol and Drug Services Coordinator.

66 Methamphetamine use not only devastates the body, but also destroys lives and tears apart families. 99

—Dave Codgill, "The Anti-Public Safety Committee," *Codgill's Capitol Corner*, January 2006.

Dave Codgill is a Republican state assembly member in California who has worked to support state funding of methamphetamine programs.

* Editor's Note: While the definition of a primary source can be narrowly or broadly defined, for the purposes of Compact Research, a primary source consists of: 1) results of original research presented by an organization or researcher; 2) eyewitness accounts of events, personal experience, or work experience; 3) first-person editorials offering pundits' opinions; 4) government officials presenting political plans and/or policies; 5) representatives of organizations presenting testimony or policy.

"The drug's impact does not stop with those who abuse methamphetamine. It victimizes innocent people through the many methamphetamine-related crimes that occur by those under the influence of this drug."

—Gary W. Oetjen, "Law Enforcement and the Fight Against Methamphetamine," *Vital Speeches of the Day*, September 15, 2006.

Gary W. Oetjen is the special agent in charge of the Drug Enforcement Administration office in Louisville, Kentucky. This quote is from a speech he delivered before Congress.

"During this time one of the reasons my daughters were looking out for me was because the police had arrested me for bad checks. . . . The authorities knew I was on meth because of the circle of people I ran with. They were always getting me for something."

—Charlotte Sanders, "I Felt Like Super Mom," Partnership for a Drug-Free America, May 5, 2006. www.drugfreeamerica.org.

Charlotte Sanders is a former methamphetamine addict.

"The most dangerous stage of meth abuse for . . . law enforcement officers is called 'tweaking.' . . . Tweakers often behave or react violently and if a tweaker is using alcohol or another depressant, his negative feelings and associated dangers intensify."

—National Drug Intelligence Center, "Heavy Meth Use and Safety," Stop Drugs. www.stopdrugs.org.

Stop Drugs is an informational organization and Web site maintained by the California attorney general's office.

> **We are beginning to realize that we can't just keep filling our jails with addicts without trying to end the cycle. . . . We have to learn more about treating meth addicts successfully.**

—Susan Gaertner, "The Sudafed Is Gone, but Meth Rages on," August 22, 2005. www.susangaertner.com.

Susan Gaertner is a county attorney in Minnesota, a state that has been heavily affected by methamphetamine abuse.

> **Officials who deal with methamphetamine abuse recognize the promise of treatment and caution against the futility of relying on prison to address methamphetamine abuse.**

—Ryan S. King, "The Next Big Thing? Methamphetamine in the United States," Sentencing Project, June 2006.

Ryan S. King is a policy analyst with the Sentencing Project. He specializes in the American criminal justice system.

> **Instead of setting up 'meth prisons,' state and federal government can fight the drug war by putting their energy towards creating drug treatment programs that work . . . so addicts can get the help they need.**

—Greg Mathis, "Why Do Meth Addicts Get Treatment While Crack Addicts Get Prison Time?" Black America Web, January 26, 2006. www.blackamericaweb.com.

Greg Mathis is a judge, civil rights activist, and vice president of Rainbow PUSH, a civil rights organization.

> **[For] reasons partly connected to methamphetamine abuse, the number of reports of child abuse has risen . . . , the number of kids going into an overstretched foster care system has gone up, and the state resources available to deal with the situation have dwindled.**

—David Sarasohn, "Child Abuse Numbers," *Oregonian*, June 4. 2006.

David Sarasohn is the associate editor of the *Oregonian* newspaper.

❝No one plans to end up in prison for methamphetamine abuse . . . no one plans for these things, I know I didn't.❞

—Aaronette Noble, testimony before the House Committee on Government Reform, June 28, 2006.

Aaronette Nobel is a former methamphetamine addict who spent time in prison for her addiction and testified before Congress about the effectiveness of treatment she has received.

❝[A] father accidentally spilled ether while manufacturing methamphetamine. . . . This resulted in a methamphetamine lab raid and the parents' four children were taken into protective custody. . . . All the children were malnourished.❞

—Frederick Aigner, statement before the Senate Committee on Finance, April 25, 2006.

Frederick Aigner is a Lutheran clergyman and president of Lutheran Social Services in Illinois.

Is There a Link Between Methamphetamine Addiction and Crime?

- In 2005 Minnesota had the highest rate of incarceration growth in the nation. Officials attribute much of that growth to methamphetamine-related crimes.

- Utah estimates that as much as 80 percent of the criminal activity in the state is related in some way to methamphetamine.

- In Denver an average of 95 percent of suspects arrested in meth cases have weapons, estimates the local Bureau of Alcohol, Tobacco, Firearms, and Explosives.

- More than 40 percent of adult men arrested in Hawaii, one of the states most affected by meth, test positive for the drug.

- A National Association of Counties (NACO) survey found that overall, counties reported a 60 percent increase in domestic violence due to meth, a 53 percent increase in assault, and a 70 percent increase in robbery.

- Forty percent of child welfare officials surveyed by NACO reported an increase in out-of-home placements in 2004 due to meth.

- Many meth-related crimes are committed by people who have no previous criminal record.

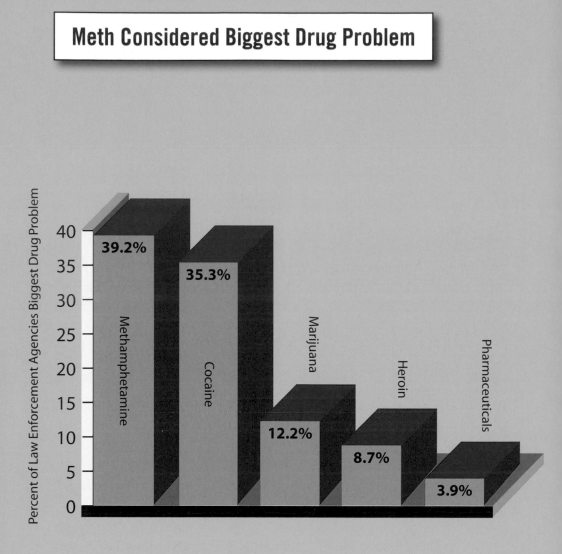

Meth Considered Biggest Drug Problem

Percent of Law Enforcement Agencies Biggest Drug Problem

- 40
- 35
- 30
- 25
- 20
- 15
- 10
- 5
- 0

Methamphetamine — **39.2%**

Cocaine — **35.3%**

Marijuana — **12.2%**

Heroin — **8.7%**

Pharmaceuticals — **3.9%**

Law enforcement officials report meth as their biggest drug problem at 39.2 percent, while cocaine comes in second at 35.3 percent. While meth use is lower than other drugs, its significant impact on crime and society makes it a top concern to law enforcement officials.

Source: U.S. Drug Enforcement Administration, National Drug Threat Assessment 2006, www.dea.gov.

Arrested Adult Males Testing Positive for Meth

This graph compares the percentage of arrested men who tested positive for meth in twenty-two heavily affected cities. Cities in the West and Midwest of the country have the highest incidence. This corresponds to the higher meth abuse rates found in those regions of the country.

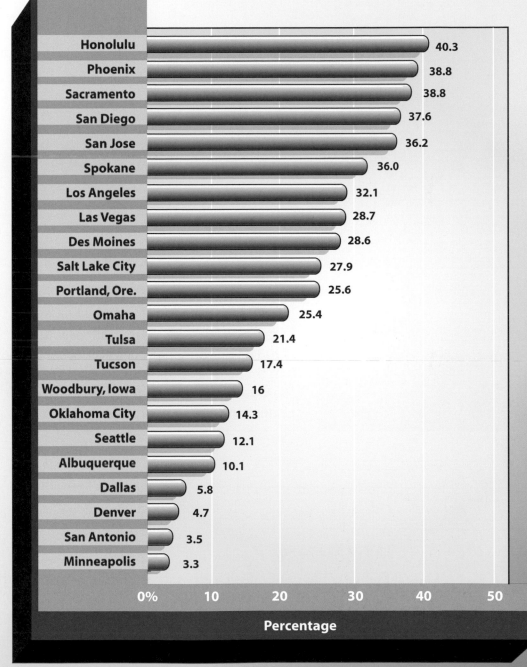

City	Percentage
Honolulu	40.3
Phoenix	38.8
Sacramento	38.8
San Diego	37.6
San Jose	36.2
Spokane	36.0
Los Angeles	32.1
Las Vegas	28.7
Des Moines	28.6
Salt Lake City	27.9
Portland, Ore.	25.6
Omaha	25.4
Tulsa	21.4
Tucson	17.4
Woodbury, Iowa	16
Oklahoma City	14.3
Seattle	12.1
Albuquerque	10.1
Dallas	5.8
Denver	4.7
San Antonio	3.5
Minneapolis	3.3

Percentage

Source: National Institute of Justice, "Arrested Adult Males Testing Positive for Meth," 2003.

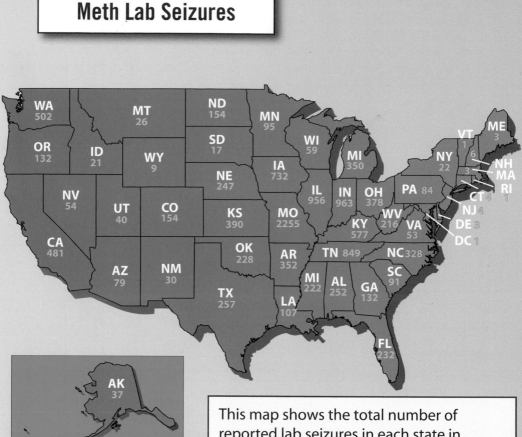

Meth Lab Seizures

WA 502
OR 132
ID 21
MT 26
WY 9
ND 154
SD 17
NE 247
MN 95
WI 59
MI 350
IA 732
NV 54
UT 40
CO 154
KS 390
MO 2255
IL 956
IN 963
OH 378
PA 84
NY 22
VT 1
ME 3
NH 6
MA 3
RI 1
CT 4
NJ 4
DE 3
DC 1
WV 216
VA 53
CA 481
AZ 79
NM 30
TX 257
OK 228
AR 352
TN 849
KY 577
NC 328
MI 222
AL 252
GA 132
SC 91
LA 107
FL 232
AK 37
HI 15

This map shows the total number of reported lab seizures in each state in 2005. Although meth use is concentrated in the West and Midwest regions, meth production is spread more evenly across the country.

Source: Kansas Methamphetamine Prevention Project, National Clandestine Laboratory Database, www.ksmeth preventionproject.org, 2006.

- Once the initial euphoria of a meth high wears off, most users experience a long "downward" period before the crash at the bottom; users tend to be most violent during this period.

- Those high on meth do not feel pain and often display unnatural strength.

- It costs an average of thirty-five hundred dollars to clean up a meth cooking site, according to the DEA.

Property and Felony Crimes Committed by Meth Addicts Doubled

This chart shows that in just two years the crime rate of meth addicts doubled. The spread of meth across the country is happening at an alarming rate. Once addicted to meth, users become desperate to find their next fix and are more likely to commit crime.

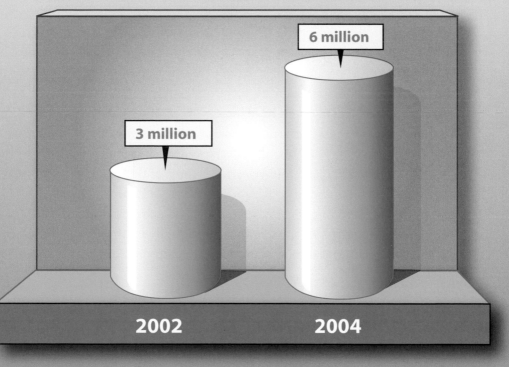

6 million

3 million

2002   2004

Source: Fight Crime: Invest in Kids, "Meth Crime Rises as Budget Axe Falls," www.fightcrime.com.

How Can Methamphetamine Addiction Be Prevented?

❝We need to take on this scourge [of methamphetamine] before it endangers more children and shatters more families across the country.❞

—Dianne Feinstein, "Will Putting Cold Medicines Behind the Counter Cut Meth Abuse?" *CQ Researcher*, July 2005.

Many groups dedicated exclusively to preventing methamphetamine use, including community organizations, treatment centers, and nonprofit organizations, have opened throughout the country during the first decade of the twenty-first century. Governments at the local, state, and federal levels have increased funding of meth-related initiatives in recent years, especially in the states most affected by the drug. Some politicians have argued that because the nation's meth problem is mostly in the western and midwestern portions of the country, Washington has yet to take the drug as seriously as the situation requires, with the White House still citing marijuana as its top drug concern. In 2005, though, Congress passed the Combat Methamphetamine Epidemic Act, sweeping federal legislation that attacks the meth problem from a variety of angles.

Many Effective Treatments Exist

Drug experts caution against exaggerating the difficulty of treating methamphetamine addiction. Despite some media reports to the contrary, meth addiction is not any easier or harder to treat than that of other drugs, such as crack and heroin. Meth addicts have about the same chance of staying clean for a year—60 percent—as other addicts do.

Traditional twelve-step programs, though, which focus on confrontation and are popular for treating alcohol and narcotics addictions, may not be as effective for meth addicts, warns UCLA neuropsychiatrist Rawson. Meth addicts tend to be violent and aggressive. The National Institute on Drug Abuse recommends a more nonconfrontational, combination treatment that teaches addicts to avoid their particular drug triggers and offers strategies for dealing with stress effectively.

Despite these cautions, Crystal Meth Anonymous groups, twelve-step programs using the same methods as Alcoholics Anonymous and Narcotics Anonymous, have formed chapters in thirty-two states. The group first began operating in New York in 1999 and has seen attendance soar. Other community-based support groups

> " **Meth addiction is not any easier or harder to treat than that of other drugs, such as crack and heroin.** "

have also become popular. One group specifically targeting addicted parents, Moms Off Meth, has sixteen chapters in the state of Iowa.

Family-based treatment, in which an entire family is included in the rehabilitation process, has proven effective. Congress considered increasing funding for the treatment during a House Government Committee meeting on methamphetamine, held in June 2006. A former meth addict testified that the treatment helped her and her husband, saying, "Our addiction tore our family apart, so we needed to find our solution as a family."[23]

States and counties have also begun to open prisons dedicated exclusively to methamphetamine addicts or those who have committed crimes related to the drug. The so-called "meth prisons" have proven effective in reducing recidivism in addicts. In traditional prisons the drug is widely available on the black market. Most addicts in these prisons will continue using while incarcerated. In the meth prisons special monitoring keeps the black market supply to a minimum. In addition, all of the facilities include intensive treatment and rehabilitation programs helpful to nonviolent drug offenders.

Media Campaigns Aid Prevention Efforts

As meth addiction has grown, nonprofit organizations have responded with large-scale public awareness campaigns meant to educate the public about the dangers of the drug. In San Francisco, local government has sponsored posters and ads with catchy slogans encouraging gay men to avoid "crystal mess."[24] Partnership for a Drug-Free America, a national nonprofit organization, began its first large-scale public relations program targeted specifically at methamphetamine prevention in March 2006.

Many of these organizations utilize the graphic nature of the drug's effects to turn people off. In the state of Montana, software billionaire Thomas Siebel has spent $5.6 million of his own fortune on billboards, radio ads, and television spots with striking depictions of the effects of meth use. One ad shows a teenager high on meth plucking out her entire eyebrow, hair by hair. On highway billboards photographs of the rotting teeth and gums of meth users are blown up to fifty feet tall.

In Oregon a sheriff's deputy has collected a series of mug shots of meth addicts booked in his jail. The photos show users at the beginning of their addiction, when they were first brought in for

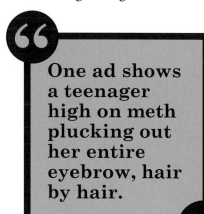

> One ad shows a teenager high on meth plucking out her entire eyebrow, hair by hair.

meth-related crimes and a few years later. The differences in the faces are so striking that the photographs have been broadcast by national media outlets and in newsmagazines. One set of photos in particular stands out. In the first picture a young woman with long brown hair stares at the camera. She does not look happy, but she does look healthy. She has fresh skin, white teeth, and a pretty, round face. The second photo, taken only a few years later, shows a woman who appears to be ten or twenty years older. Her skin is wrinkled and hangs from her face, her cheeks are sunken, and her skin is covered in sores. Her hair, neatly combed in the first picture, is a mess. But even more noticeable is the change in her expression. Her mouth hangs open somewhat, revealing that most of her teeth are gone, and her stare is vacant and glazed.

Restricting Sales of Meth Ingredients

Efforts to prevent methamphetamine addiction must also include controlling the supply of methamphetamine available. For many state governments this has meant placing restrictions on over-the-counter drugs containing pseudoephedrine or ephedrine, meth's key ingredients. In part, the insidious nature of the drug is due to the wide availability of these chemicals and of the tools for making the drug.

As of the time of this writing in 2006, thirty-five states had responded to this problem by placing at least some controls on medicines with the key ingredients. By far the strictest control was passed in August 2006 by the state of Oregon, which now requires a prescription for all pseudoephedrine or ephedrine-containing drugs. Other states, such as Missouri, have taken the serious but less drastic measure of reclassifying pseudoephedrine and ephedrine as Schedule V drugs, the same classifications as some cough syrups containing the mild narcotic codeine. Pharmacists have the right to require customers to sign a logbook when purchasing drugs with this classification and to restrict how much they can buy at one time. Arkansas, for instance, limits the grams of pseudoephedrine-containing medicine a customer can buy per month. Other states have begun selling the drugs from a locked case, as cigarettes are sold. After implementing these measures, some states have reported up to a 90 percent drop in meth lab seizures by law enforcement. The cooks are no longer able to easily obtain the raw ingredients needed to make the drug. They suspend operations, either temporarily or permanently, and police do not encounter as many labs.

> " Oregon . . . now requires a prescription for all pseudoephedrine or ephedrine-containing drugs. "

Even in states without official limits on pseudoephedrine and ephedrine, some major pharmacy chains such as Rite Aid, Target, K-Mart, and Wal-Mart, have voluntarily placed cold medicines and decongestants behind their counters and limited customer purchases. While these efforts have limited meth production, they have also forced meth cooks to get creative. Addicts hired by cooks go from pharmacy to pharmacy, buying their allotted two or three packs of Sudafed or Claritin. They punch the pills out of the blister packs until they have enough for a batch of meth. These addicts are often called "Smurfers," because they are gatherers, like the blue cartoon characters Smurfs.

Increased Demand for Foreign Chemicals

State legislatures and retail chains have encountered heavy opposition to these measures from drug companies and their lobbying groups such as the Consumer Healthcare Products Association. Regular consumers who just want some allergy relief or who have a cold should not have to sign a logbook or get a prescription, they argue.

Some drug companies, though, are seeking to eliminate the problem by creating new products that do not contain the restricted chemicals. Pharmaceutical giant Pfizer has begun making the popular decongestant Sudafed with a new ingredient called phenylephrine. Historically though, this type of attempt has proven futile in diverting meth cooks. In previous years ephedrine was the chemical of choice for cooks. Companies stopped using it in their products and switched to its cousin, pseudoephedrine. Meth makers followed suit, developing new recipes and techniques for the new chemical. Methamphetamine made from phenylephrine has not yet been developed, but cooks have proven their ingenuity when it comes to adapting to new ingredients.

> " **Sixty-five to 80 percent of methamphetamine comes from Mexico** "

With all of the tightening of domestic chemicals, however, some experts worry that the market for foreign-made pseudoephedrine and ephedrine will only increase. Small-time meth labs and meth cooks are only a percentage of the nation's supply. Sixty-five to 80 percent of methamphetamine comes from Mexico, where the drug is manufactured in giant superlabs. In 2005 Anthony Placido, a high-ranking DEA official, told Congress that "perhaps the greatest emerging drug threat from Mexico is the production of methamphetamine for sale and use in the United States."[25] Controlling the international flow of meth's raw ingredients has become a major concern for the federal government in the twenty-first century.

Monitoring of Ingredients

Since the Drug Enforcement Administration first identified methamphetamine abuse as a problem in the early 1980s, the federal government has addressed the issue through funding and legislation in incremental steps. The DEA increased its meth budget from $127.5 million in 2001 to $151.4 million in 2004. In Congress, representatives have formed a "meth caucus" among themselves. The members of the caucus focus specifically on promoting legislation to combat the meth problem. Since its inception, the meth caucus has grown from 4 members in 2000 to 118 in 2005. By far though, Congress took its most aggressive step in November 2005 with the passage of the Combat Methamphetamine Epidemic Act.

In addition to increasing penalties for meth offenders and cooks and supporting states' retail restrictions, this legislation signified the first time the United States has reached out to the international community for assistance in combating the methamphetamine problem. Trafficking in the drug has increased on every continent in the world, most of it in the form of raw pseudoephedrine and ephedrine. The House Committee on Government Reform summed up the essence of the problem in a December 2005 report:

> **The DEA increased its meth budget from $127.5 million in 2001 to $151.4 million in 2004.**

> Most of our meth problem can be attributed to one simple fact: The United States and the international community have failed to set up an effective control system for pseudoephedrine and other precursor chemical products. . . . Many nations are importing far more than they can legitimately consume, meaning the excess is probably being diverted to meth production.[26]

The Combat Meth Act increases the government's authority to monitor the import and export of these chemicals in foreign countries and withholds aid from countries that do not cooperate. In March 2006 the International Narcotics Control Board, an independent body, confirmed the necessity of monitoring the chemical supply. It issued a statement that countries need to report ephedrine and pseudoephedrine demand so that smuggling can be located.

Monitoring the world's supply of ephedrine and pseudoephedrine should be easy, in theory. Only nine factories worldwide manufacture the chemicals in Germany, the Czech Republic, China, and India. But until 2006 the orders and shipments where virtually untracked. With the increasing awareness of trafficking, China, Germany, and India now notify the International Narcotics Control Board before shipping the chemicals, enabling the board to match various countries' imports against their legitimate demand.

Continued Control Is Needed

The United States has expressed support for an international global intelligence network coordinated among all countries that import or export any amount of pseudoephedrine or ephedrine. The network would monitor shipments and compare demand with import and export data to stop traffickers. The struggle to prevent methamphetamine addiction has been deeply affected by the ability of cooks to make the drug with different ingredients, however.

> The struggle to prevent methamphetamine addiction has been deeply affected by the ability of cooks to make the drug with different ingredients.

As controls on ephedrine and pseudoephedrine have tightened worldwide, Chinese suppliers have begun using the herb ephedra, also called ma huang, to make meth. Ephedra contains small amounts of ephedrine that can be extracted to make the drug. The ephedra is shipped into Mexico from China for manufacture there into meth and has begun making its way into the United States. Ephedra is not an ideal ingredient, however. It grows wild and must be gathered by hand. In addition, it takes twenty-five times as much ephedra to make methamphetamine as it does using raw ephedrine or pseudoephedrine. Mexican meth made from ephedra still is not commonly found in the United States.

The difficulty in preventing methamphetamine addiction does not lie in the actual treatment of meth addicts. A meth habit is neither easier nor harder to break than addictions to other, similar substances. The difficulty is in controlling the supply of the completed drug and its raw ingredients. The vigilance and cooperation of the world community in monitoring the flow of raw ingredients is the key to methamphetamine addiction prevention.

How Can Methamphetamine Addiction Be Prevented?

66 For several months now, Montana kids have seen graphic . . . accounts of meth abuse, through a series of ads run by businessman Tom Siebel. . . . The ads are having an effect. 99

—Max Baucus, statement before the Senate Finance Committee, April 25, 2006.

Max Baucus is a Democratic senator from Montana.

66 The methamphetamine threat cannot be defeated without better control of precursor chemicals, like ephedrine and pseudoephedrine. . . . [Criminals divert methamphetamine ingredients] at the retail, whole-sale, and international levels, requiring a comprehensive plan to stop diversion at each of these levels. 99

—Alberto Gonzales, quoted in "Bush Administration Calls for Enhanced Controls on Ingredients Used to Make Meth," Office of National Drug Control Policy, May 23, 2005.

Alberto Gonzales is the U.S. attorney general for the Bush administration.

* Editor's Note: While the definition of a primary source can be narrowly or broadly defined, for the purposes of Compact Research, a primary source consists of: 1) results of original research presented by an organization or researcher; 2) eyewitness accounts of events, personal experience, or work experience; 3) first-person editorials offering pundits' opinions; 4) government officials presenting political plans and/or policies; 5) representatives of organizations presenting testimony or policy.

" By making it more difficult to purchase large quantities of cold medicine blister packs . . . it will be far tougher for meth cooks to make this devastating drug."

—Dianne Feinstein, "Drug Store Chains Join Feinstein-Talent Battle Against Meth," News from Senator Feinstein, May 2, 2005. http://feinstein.senate.gov.

Dianne Feinstein is a Democratic senator from California who has supported antimethamphetamine legislation.

" Recent proposals [that] . . . advocate only allowing pseudoephedrine to be sold in pharmacies . . . will place unnecessary burdens on pharmacies while at the same time limiting consumer access to these medicines."

—John A. Gilbert, "Will Putting Cold Medicines Behind the Counter Cut Meth Abuse?" *CQ Researcher*, July 2005.

John A. Gilbert is a former attorney for the Drug Enforcement Administration. He specializes in food and drug law in his private practice.

" [The children of addicts] . . . demand . . . the hassle of a few extra minutes at the pharmacy waiting for the cold medicine that drug cookers turn into meth."

— *Portland Oregonian*, "The Little Round Faces of Meth," July 9, 2005.

The *Oregonian* newspaper, based in Portland, Oregon, is responsible for award-winning coverage of methamphetamine by reporter Steve Suo and others.

" Allergy and cold remedies containing pseudoephedrine, a chemical that can illegally be used to make meth, must now be locked behind the counter. . . . It's unclear that there are any net benefits."

—John Tierney, "Potheads and Sudafed," *New York Times*, April 25, 2006.

John Tierney is a *New York Times* columnist who writes about science, economics, and technology.

❝Perhaps the greatest emerging drug threat from Mexico is the production of methamphetamine for sale and use in the United States.❞

—Anthony Placido, remarks before the House Government Reform Committee, Subcommittee on Criminal Justice, Drug Policy and Human Resources, June 14, 2005.

Anthony Placido is chief of intelligence at the Drug Enforcement Administration.

❝Law enforcement needs help in shutting off the drug's flow from Mexico and the Southwest. And Congress has helped by ordering cold remedies with pseudo-ephedrine . . . off store shelves in the few states that hadn't done so.❞

—*Omaha World-Herald*, "Meth Remains a Major Problem in the Midlands, Even If the Rest of the Nation Got the Warning," June 27, 2006.

The *Omaha World-Herald* is Nebraska's primary local newspaper. It has a circulation of approximately one hundred ninety thousand.

❝[The Combat Methamphetamine Epidemic Act] introduces common-sense safeguards that would make many of the ingredients used in manufacturing meth harder to obtain in bulk and easier for law enforcement to track.❞

—George W. Bush, "President Signs USA Patriot Improvement and Reauthorization Act," Office of the Press Secretary, March 9, 2006.

George W. Bush is the forty-third president of the United States. In March 2006 he signed a large-scale methamphetamine control bill into law.

66 [Making meth] requires chemicals made at just nine factories around the world. . . . Control these nine factories, and you cure the meth epidemic. 99

—*San Diego Union-Tribune*, "Meth's Ray of Hope," July 1, 2006.

The *San Diego Union-Tribune* is the second oldest newspaper in Southern California. It has won two Pulitzer Prizes for excellence in journalism.

66 Methamphetamine trafficking and the movement of its chemicals are now a global epidemic. 99

— Karen P. Tandy, speech delivered at the National Methamphetamine Chemicals Initiative Conference, May 18, 2006.

Karen P. Tandy is administrator of the Drug Enforcement Administration.

66 The United States . . . must work more closely with our international partners to restrict the global diversion of the precursor chemicals used to make synthetic drugs. 99

—John P. Walters, public statement, Office of National Drug Control Policy, March 17, 2006.

John P. Walters is director of the White House Office of National Drug Control Policy.

How Can Methamphetamine Addiction Be Prevented?

- Requests for treatment for meth abuse have jumped 420 percent in recent years, according to the National Association of Counties.

- Relapse rates for methamphetamine use are similar to those for cocaine and heroin.

- Twelve-step programs aimed at meth users have proven only somewhat effective.

- Oregon was the first state to make the precursor chemical pseudoephedrine available only by prescription.

- According to *Newsweek* magazine, the recidivism rate for former meth addicts released from "meth prisons" was 50 percent less than among those released from regular prisons.

- Mexican superlabs can produce one hundred thousand doses of meth in a single cooking.

- Mexico imports 224 tons of pseudoephedrine a year. It legitimately needs only 130 tons of the ingredient, according to the *Economist*.

- In 2004 U.S. authorities seized 174 tons of illegally imported pseudoephedrine. Legally imported pseudoephedrine was only 600 tons, the *Oregonian* newspaper reported in March 2006.

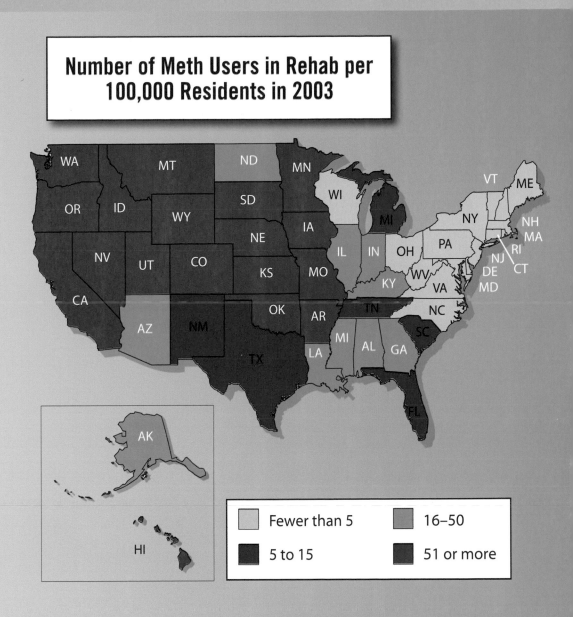

Number of Meth Users in Rehab per 100,000 Residents in 2003

Legend:
- Fewer than 5
- 5 to 15
- 16–50
- 51 or more

This map shows the number of meth users who have entered drug treatment programs or rehabilitation centers by state throughout the nation. The numbers are for the most part parallel with states' overall rate of methamphetamine abuse.

Source: *Frontline*, "The Meth Epidemic," Number of Meth Users in Rehab per 100,000 Residents in 2003, 2006. www.pbs.org.

- Methamphetamine abuse was not a problem in the United Kingdom until 2006.

- The Drug Enforcement Administration increased its meth budget from $127.5 million in 2001 to $151.4 million in 2004.

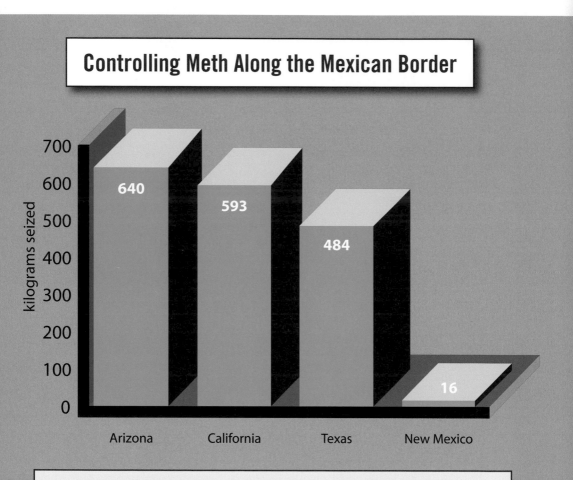

Controlling Meth Along the Mexican Border

This graph shows the amount of illegal meth seized by federal authorities at major ports of entry in the United States along the Mexican border for one year. Arizona leads the list at 640 kilograms, while New Mexico had only 16 kilograms seized. Restricting the flow of illegal meth into the United States is critical to the prevention of meth abuse.

Source: El Paso Intelligence Center, "Methamphetamine Seizures at or Between Ports of Entry, in Kilograms, 2003," March 2005.

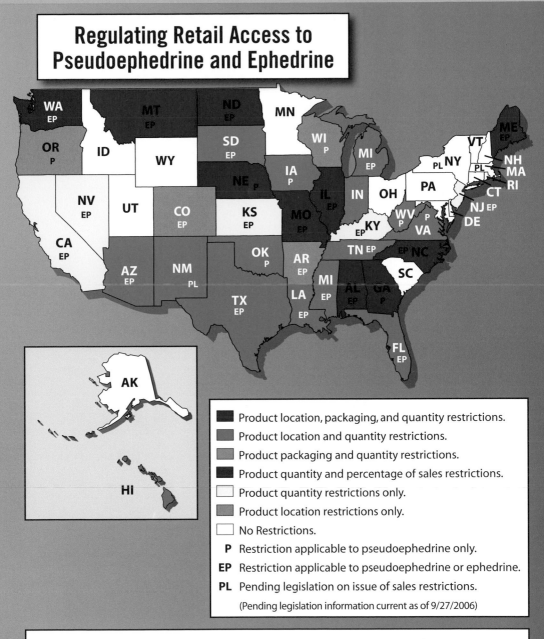

Regulating Retail Access to Pseudoephedrine and Ephedrine

WA EP
MT EP
ND EP
MN
OR P
ID
WY
SD EP
WI P
MI EP
ME EP
VT
NY
PL
NH
MA
RI
NV EP
UT
CO EP
NE P
IA P
IL EP
IN
OH
PA
CT
NJ EP
DE
CA EP
KS EP
MO EP
KY EP
WV P
VA P
AZ EP
NM PL
OK P
AR EP
TN EP
NC EP
SC
TX EP
LA EP
MI EP
AL EP
GA P
FL EP
AK
HI

Legend:

- Product location, packaging, and quantity restrictions.
- Product location and quantity restrictions.
- Product packaging and quantity restrictions.
- Product quantity and percentage of sales restrictions.
- Product quantity restrictions only.
- Product location restrictions only.
- No Restrictions.
- **P** Restriction applicable to pseudoephedrine only.
- **EP** Restriction applicable to pseudoephedrine or ephedrine.
- **PL** Pending legislation on issue of sales restrictions.

(Pending legislation information current as of 9/27/2006)

Pseudoephedrine and Ephedrine are found in many over-the-counter cold medications but can be used for meth production. This map shows the restrictions states have placed on stores regarding the sales quantity, packaging, and shelf location of products containing ephedrine and pseudoephedrine. The restrictions were put in place to reduce the number of operating meth labs.

Source: Rhea Arledge, National District Attorneys Association, "Methamphetamine: Efforts to Stem the Tide of Clandestine Methamphetamine Laboratories," 2005. www.ndaa.org.

Key People and Advocacy Groups

Jesus, Adan, and **Luis Amezcua** are Mexican drug kingpins believed to have created the methamphetamine superlab system capable of standardized, large-scale meth manufacture. The brothers ran a successful meth cartel until the late 1990s when they were arrested and sent to prison. The cartel is still operating under the direction of the Amezcuas from prison, authorities believe.

Brian Baird is a Democratic congressional representative from the state of Washington who cofounded the Congressional Caucus to Fight and Control Methamphetamine. Baird also was a cosponsor in the House of the Combat Methamphetamine Epidemic Act, comprehensive federal legislation to control and prevent illegal methamphetamine use.

Chen Bingxi is one of the world's biggest manufacturers of illegal drugs. His organization is accused of making over twelve tons of crystal methamphetamine worth more than $5.5 billion. Bingxi was arrested in 2003 and went on trial in China in March 2005.

Carol Falkowski is the director of research communications at the Hazelden Foundation, a drug treatment and research center in Minnesota. She is considered an expert on drug abuse trends and frequently appears on television and radio to discuss the nation's methamphetamine problem. She has produced two television documentaries about methamphetamine addiction.

Dianne Feinstein is a Democratic senator from California, and was the creator and cosponsor of the Combat Methamphetamine Epidemic Act along with Republican senator Jim Talent. Feinstein also introduced the Methamphetamine Control Act in 1996, one of the first pieces of federal methamphetamine legislation.

Gene Haislip is a former Drug Enforcement Administration administrator who is credited with recognizing the dangerous potential of methamphetamine's precursor chemicals as early as the 1980s. Haislip urged the federal government to monitor supplies of ephedrine and encountered stiff resistance from the pharmaceutical industry. He has continued to serve as a consultant for drug manufacturers in their efforts to control precursor chemicals.

Richard Rawson is a neuropsychiatrist who has studied methamphetamine addiction for over twenty years. He is associate director of UCLA's Integrated Substance Abuse Center and has developed a new and effective meth addiction treatment program called the Matrix Model that combines aspects of different therapies. Rawson writes and speaks extensively on the physical effects of methamphetamine on the brain.

Thomas Siebel is the founder of the Montana Meth Project, a massive public awareness campaign to combat methamphetamine addiction. A software company executive, Siebel contributed $5.6 million of his own fortune to the project, which uses graphic images and stories to discourage potential meth users.

Steven Suo is a reporter for the *Oregonian* newspaper who was responsible for the paper's 2004 series on methamphetamine. Suo was the first to make the connection between the level of meth addiction and the corresponding purity of the nation's meth supply. Suo's findings contributed to the passage of the federal Combat Methamphetamine Epidemic Act. He was nominated for a Pulitzer Prize for his reporting on meth.

Jim Talent is a Republican senator from Missouri, has made fighting methamphetamine one of the main issues of his term. He was a cosponsor with Senator Dianne Feinstein of the Combat Methamphetamine Epidemic Act. He is also cochair of the Senate Anti-Meth Caucus and has campaigned for significant federal funding to be given to family-based methamphetamine treatment centers.

Nora Volkow is the head of the National Institute on Drug Abuse (NIDA), a federal agency that is part of the National Institutes of Health. Volkow is a medical doctor and expert on dopamine in the brain. She has made the study of methamphetamine abuse a key component of her tenure and has increased NIDA funding of meth research by 150 percent since 2003.

Susan York is the founder and executive director of Lead on America, a nonprofit organization that identifies and works to shut down methamphetamine labs in communities across the country. York created the grassroots group after living next door to a meth lab in Seattle. As of 2006, Lead on America had helped to close thirty-eight meth houses.

Chronology

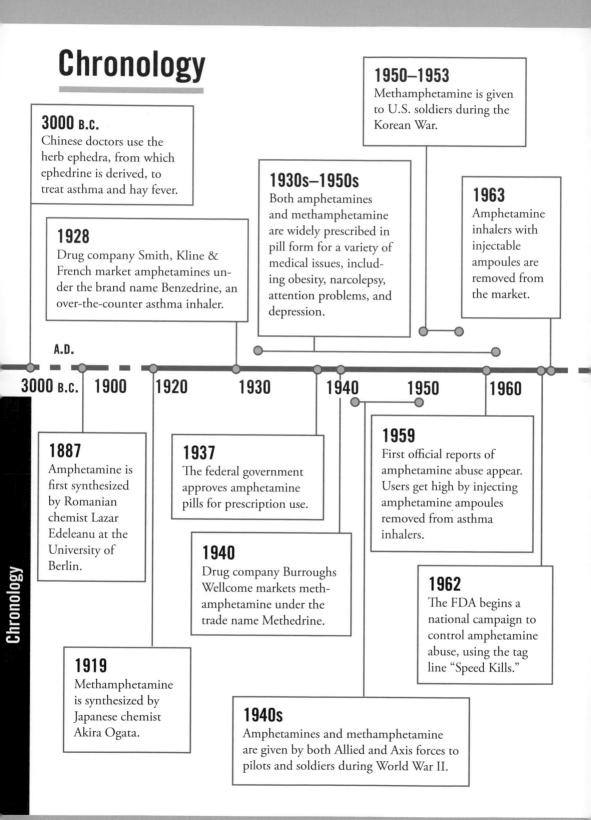

1950–1953
Methamphetamine is given to U.S. soldiers during the Korean War.

3000 B.C.
Chinese doctors use the herb ephedra, from which ephedrine is derived, to treat asthma and hay fever.

1930s–1950s
Both amphetamines and methamphetamine are widely prescribed in pill form for a variety of medical issues, including obesity, narcolepsy, attention problems, and depression.

1963
Amphetamine inhalers with injectable ampoules are removed from the market.

1928
Drug company Smith, Kline & French market amphetamines under the brand name Benzedrine, an over-the-counter asthma inhaler.

A.D.

| 3000 B.C. | 1900 | 1920 | 1930 | 1940 | 1950 | 1960 |

1887
Amphetamine is first synthesized by Romanian chemist Lazar Edeleanu at the University of Berlin.

1937
The federal government approves amphetamine pills for prescription use.

1959
First official reports of amphetamine abuse appear. Users get high by injecting amphetamine ampoules removed from asthma inhalers.

1940
Drug company Burroughs Wellcome markets methamphetamine under the trade name Methedrine.

1962
The FDA begins a national campaign to control amphetamine abuse, using the tag line "Speed Kills."

1919
Methamphetamine is synthesized by Japanese chemist Akira Ogata.

1940s
Amphetamines and methamphetamine are given by both Allied and Axis forces to pilots and soldiers during World War II.

1970s
Meth gains popularity among West Coast motorcycle gangs who both smuggle the drug and use it. Meth is nicknamed "crank" for the bikers' penchant for hiding the drug in their motorcycles' crankcases.

1990s
Methamphetamine begins spread beyond the West Coast into the Southwest and Midwest. Crystal meth gains popularity in the gay communities of California.

2005
Congress passes the Combat Methamphetamine Epidemic Act, restricting the sale of ephedrine and pseudoephedrine and strengthening meth-related penalties.

1982
The Drug Enforcement Administration puts controls on phenyl-2-propanone, the key ingredient needed to make amphetamine.

2004
The Office of National Drug Control Policy releases the National Synthetic Drug Action Plan, making numerous recommendations for the control and prevention of methamphetamine abuse.

1970   **1980**   **1990**   **2000**   **2005**

1971
Amphetamine and methamphetamine are classified as Schedule II drugs by the FDA, meaning they have some therapeutic uses and high potential for abuse.

2000
U.S. representative Brian Baird founds the bipartisan Congressional Caucus to Fight and Control Methamphetamine to draft meth-related legislation.

1993
Legislation restricting the sale of pills containing ephedrine is passed. Meth cooks switch to pseudoephedrine, which remains unregulated.

1996
Congress passes the first large-scale methamphetamine legislation, the Comprehensive Methamphetamine Control Act.

1970
Amphetamine and methamphetamine are declared illegal without a prescription as outlined in the Comprehensive Drug Abuse Prevention and Control Act passed by Congress.

1995
Large-scale production of methamphetamine begins in Mexico. Mexican meth enters the U.S. market through cocaine channels.

2006
Oregon becomes the first state to make all drugs containing ephedrine and pseudoephedrine, including cold medicines, available by prescription only.

Related Organizations

Chicago Crystal Meth Task Force
411 S. Wells St., Suite 300
Chicago, IL 60607
phone: (312) 922-2322
fax: (312) 922-2916
e-mail: policy@aids.chicago.org
Web site: www.crystalbreaks.org

The Crystal Meth Task Force is a program of the AIDS Foundation of Chicago aimed at disseminating information about the dangers of crystal meth to the gay community. The task force is centered around a public awareness campaign and Web site titled "Crystal Breaks."

Crystal Meth Anonymous
8205 Santa Monica Blvd.
West Hollywood, CA 90046
phone: (213) 488-4455
Web site: www.crystalmeth.org

Crystal Meth Anonymous is a twelve-step program that provides a system for meth addicts who want to quit. The program closely resembles other twelve-step programs, such as Alcoholics Anonymous, and requires that its members attend weekly meetings and take responsibility for their actions, among other things.

Drug Reform Coordination Network (DRCnet)
1623 Connecticut Ave. NW, 3rd Fl.
Washington, DC 20009
phone: (202) 293-8340 fax: (202) 293-88344
e-mail: drcnet@drcnet.org
Web site: www.stopthedrugwar.org

DRCnet is a nonprofit organization that supports the legalization of all drugs, including methamphetamine. The group maintains the online Schaffer Library of Drug Policy that provides archived material related to drug policy reform.

Erowid

PO Box 1116
Grass Valley, CA 95945
e-mail: sage@erowid.org
Web site: www.erowid.org

Erowid is a nonprofit group that provides extensive information on the chemical composition, manufacturing, and use of psychoactive drugs. The group does not take any sort of moral stance on drugs but aims merely to provide factual information. Erowid offers most of its material on its Web site.

KCI: The Anti-Meth Site

e-mail: kcimeth@yahoo.com
Web site: www.kci.org

KCI is a privately funded nonprofit organization whose mission is to maintain an extensive Web site that provides information on the dangers of methamphetamine use. The site offers tips on how to avoid the drug and links to treatment programs and social services for methamphetamine addicts, in addition to a message board and testimonials from former users.

Law Enforcement Against Prohibition (LEAP)

121 Mystic Ave.
Medford, MA 02155
phone: (781) 393-6985
e-mail: info@leap.cc
Web site: http://leap.cc

LEAP is a nonprofit organization consisting of former and current law enforcement officers who work to end the current drug policy in the United States. The group works to end the current violence and self-harm that characterize the "War on Drugs" by advocating for the legalization and monitoring of all drugs, including methamphetamine.

Lead on America

PO Box 6321
Lynnwood, WA 98036
phone: (425) 299-0334
e-mail: susan@leadonamerica.org

Web site: www.leadonamerica.org

Lead on America is a grassroots organization based in the Northwest that supports citizens wishing to end illegal methamphetamine activity in their communities. Lead on America facilitates between law enforcement and community members and provides information for those wishing to help close local meth houses.

Meth Watch

900 Nineteenth St. NW, Suite 700
Washington, DC 20006
phone: (202) 429-9260
fax: (202) 223-6835
e-mail: eassey@chpa-info.org
Web site: www.methwatch.com

Meth Watch is a program aimed at reducing the illegal sale of methamphetamine's raw ingredients by increasing retailers' awareness of suspicious buying behavior. The Consumer Healthcare Products Association, a pharmaceutical lobbying group, sponsors the program, which encourages collaboration between retailers and law enforcement.

National Institute of Drug Abuse (NIDA)

6001 Executive Blvd., Rm. 5213
Bethesda, MD 20892
phone: (301) 443-1124
e-mail: information@nida.nih.gov
Web site: www.nida.nih.gov

NIDA is a federal institution that is part of the National Institutes of Health, which are a subsidiary of the Department of Health and Human Services. NIDA's focus is the scientific study of drug abuse and accompanying trends. The institute also provides funding for individuals and institutions conducting research on drug abuse.

Office of National Drug Control Policy (ONDCP)

750 Seventeenth St.
Washington, DC 20503
phone: (800) 666-3332
fax: (301) 519-5212

e-mail: ondcp@ncjrs.org

Web site: www.whitehousedrugpolicy.org

The ONDCP is the White House's drug policy arm. The office implements the president's drug policy initiatives and communicates with the public about pertinent drug control issues. The ONDCP maintains numerous documents at its Web site, including archived policy reports as well as practical material for parents, community leaders, and educators.

Partnership for a Drug-Free America

405 Lexington Ave., Suite 1601

New York, NY 10174

phone: (212) 922-1560

fax: (212) 922-1570

Web site: www.drugfreeamerica.org

The Partnership for a Drug-Free America is a nonprofit organization that works to end drug abuse among teenagers and children, mainly through public service announcements and print campaigns. The privately funded group works closely with media sources to spread its antidrug message.

Tweaker.org

3180 Eighteenth St., Suite 202,

San Francisco, CA 94110

phone: (415) 502-1999

fax: (415) 502-5764

e-mail: info@tweaker.org

Web site: www.tweaker.org

Tweaker.org is a subgroup of the Stonewall Project, a gay rights organization. The group was founded to educate gay men about the increased risk of HIV transmission with crystal meth use. The group's mission states specifically that it neither promotes nor discourages meth use, aiming merely to provide information. The organization is centered around its Web site, which provides testimonials about crystal meth, both laudatory and cautionary, as well as resources for meth addicts wishing to stop.

For Further Research

Books

Sterling R. Braswell, *American Meth: A History of the Methamphetamine Epidemic in America.* Lincoln, NE: iUniverse, 2006.

Kenneth Cimino, *The Politics of Crystal Meth: Gay Men Share Stories of Addiction and Recovery.* Boca Raton, FL: Universal, 2005.

Larry R. Erdmann, *Methamphetamine: The Drug of Death.* Lincoln, NE: iUniverse, 2006.

Mary Holley, *Crystal Meth: They Call It 'Ice.'* Mustang, OK: Tate, 2005.

Dirk Johnson, *Meth: The Home-Cooked Menace.* Center City, MN: Hazelden, 2005.

Steven Lee, *Overcoming Crystal Meth Addiction: An Essential Guide to Getting Clean.* New York: Marlowe, 2006.

Duncan Osborne, *Suicide Tuesday: Gay Men and the Crystal Meth Scare.* New York: Carroll & Graf, 2005.

Frank Owen, *No Speed Limit: Meth Across America.* New York: St. Martin's, 2006.

James N. Parker and Philip M. Parker, *Methamphetamines: A Medical Dictionary, Bibliography, and Annotated Research Guide to Internet References.* San Diego: Icon Health References, 2004.

Frank Sanello, *Tweakers: How Crystal Meth Is Ravaging Gay America.* Los Angeles: Alyson, 2005.

Periodicals

Garry Boulard, "The Meth Menace," *State Legislatures,* May 2005.

Economist, "Instant Pleasure, Instant Ageing," June 18, 2005.

Rachel Halliburton, "Crystal Clear Danger," *New Statesman,* February 28, 2005.

Christopher Heredia, "Dance of Death: Crystal Meth Fuels HIV," *San Francisco Gate,* May 4, 2003.

Beth Herskovits, "Group Aims to Curb Meth Abuse with Community-Tailored Effort," *PR Week,* March 27, 2006.

David J. Jefferson, "America's Most Dangerous Drug," *Newsweek,* August 8, 2005.

David C. Lewis, "Doctors Call In Media to Shun 'Meth Baby' Myth," *Alcoholism & Drug Abuse Weekly*, August 8, 2005.

Richard Lovette and Tyler Cabot, "What It Feels Like to Do Meth," *Esquire,* August 2005.

Alexandra Marks, "A Growing Force Against Meth Use," *Christian Science Monitor,* May 3, 2005.

Andrew Murr and Sarah Childress, "A New Menace on the Rez," *Newsweek,* September 27, 2004.

Janelle Nanos, "Cold Medicine Cops," *New York*, May 22, 2006.

Andrea Neal, "Drug War: An American Epidemic," *Saturday Evening Post*, January/February 2006.

New Scientist, "A Concise Guide to Mind-Altering Drugs," November 13, 2004.

Gary W. Oetjen, "Law Enforcement and the Fight Against Methamphetamine," *Vital Speeches of the Day,* September 15, 2005.

Pamela M. Prah, "Methamphetamine," *CQ Researcher*, July 15, 2005.

Peter Provet, "The Marketplace of Meth: Spotting the Tipping Point," *Alcoholism & Drug Abuse Weekly*, August 22, 2005.

David Sheff, "My Addicted Son," *New York Times Magazine*, February 6, 2005.

Catharine Skipp and Adrian Campo-Flores, "Addiction: A 'Meth Prison' Movement," *Newsweek,* April 24, 2006.

Michael Specter, "Higher Risk," *New Yorker,* May 23, 2005.

Seth Stern, "White Powder," *CQ Weekly*, June 5, 2006.

Mark T. Sullivan, "Meth Wars," *Outdoor Life,* April 2006.

Joseph A. Troncale, "Understanding the 'Methedemic,'" *Behavioral Health Management,* September/October 2005.

Internet Sources

Common Sense for Drug Policy, "Methamphetamine Focus," July 20, 2006. www.csdp.org.

Erowid, "Methamphetamine," July 23, 2006. www.erowid.org.

Frontline, "The Meth Epidemic," PBS, 2006. www.pbs.org.

MethResources, "Overview." www.methresources.gov.

Montana Meth Project, "Real Stories," www.montanameth.org.

National Institute on Drug Abuse Research Report, "Methamphetamine Abuse and Addiction," February 8, 2005. www.nida.nih.gov.

Source Notes

Overview

1. Richard Lovette, "What It Feels Like to Do Meth," *Esquire*, August 2005.
2. Steve Duin, "'You Pretty Much Live in Darkness,'" *Portland Oregonian*, February 13, 2005.
3. Jon Bonne, "Hooked in the Haight," *MSNBC.com*, 2006.
4. Mark T. Sullivan, "Meth Wars," *Outdoor Life*, April 2006.
5. Philip Johnston, "UN Alert on Sex and Dance Drug," *Daily Telegraph* (London), March 1, 2006.

Is There a Methamphetamine Epidemic Today?

6. Office of National Drug Control Policy, "National Synthetic Drugs Action Plan," October 2004.
7. U.S. Newswire, "Prepared Remarks of Attorney General Alberto R. Gonzales at the Portland Business Alliance," March 30, 2006.
8. Quoted in Andrea Neal, "Drug War: An American Epidemic," *Saturday Evening Post*, January/February 2006.
9. Garry Boulard, "Meth Menace," *State Legislatures*, May 2005.
10. Chad Graham, "Back from the Brink," *Advocate*, September 27, 2005.
11. Sarah McCann, "Meth Ravages Lives in Northern Counties," *Minneapolis Star Tribune*, November 17, 2004.
12. Quoted in Christopher Heredia, "Dance of Death," *San Francisco Gate*, May 4, 2003.
13. Quoted in Alan Travis, "Crystal Meth to Get Class A Listing in Bid to Limit Use," *Guardian* (Manchester), June 12, 2006.

How Dangerous Is Methamphetamine Use?

14. Robert M. Brandjord, statement of the American Dental Association at the National Town Hall on Methamphetamine Awareness and Prevention, January 23, 2006.
15. Quoted in Joseph Rose, "The Faces of Meth," *Portland Oregonian*, December 28, 2004.
16. Heredia, "Dance of Death."

Is There a Link Between Methamphetamine Addiction and Crime?

17. Quoted in Andrew Buncombe, "The Crystal Craze," *Independent* (London), April 21, 2006.
18. Lovette, "What It Feels Like to Do Meth."
19. Quoted in Nancy Lofholm, "Deadly Mix of Meth, Weapons Troubles Officers," *Denver Post*, May 23, 2006.
20. Quoted in Stop Drugs, "Heavy Meth Use and Safety." www.stopdrugs.org.
21. Maia Szalavitz, "Is Meth America's

Number One Drug Problem?" Stats.org, July 19, 2006. www. stats.org.

22. Greg Mathis, "Why Do Meth Addicts Get Treatment While Crack Addicts Get Prison Time?" Black America Web, January 26, 2006. www.black americaweb.com.

How Can Methamphetamine Addiction Be Prevented?

23. Aaronette Noble, testimony before the House Committee on Government Reform, June 28, 2006.

24. Quoted in David J. Jefferson, "Party, Play—and Pay," *Newsweek,* February 28, 2005.

25. Quoted in Pamela M. Prah, "Methamphetamine," *CQ Researcher,* July 15, 2005.

26. Quoted in Steve Suo, "World Wakes Up to Meth," *Portland Oregonian,* February 14, 2006.

List of Illustrations

Index

About the Author

Emma Carlson Berne has written and edited over a dozen books for children and young adults, including biographies of Christopher Columbus and the rapper Snoop Dogg. She holds a master's degree in composition and rhetoric from Miami University in Oxford, Ohio. Emma is currently at work on a book on global warming, also for ReferencePoint Press.